Benny Hill, David Jason, Victoria Wood, Dave Allen – just a few of the top names in entertainment who feature in this enthralling autobiography of their agent, Richard Stone. Stone has many a revealing tale to tell from his half-century as impresario and theatrical agent. He tells us what the stars are really like without the greasepaint, and how they feel when their show is a fabulous success – or an unmitigated disaster.

Looking back to the days when the show at the end of the pier was the highlight of the great British seaside holiday, Stone tells of the artistes who struggled up and slipped down the greasy pole of success. He had to cope with backstage disaster, empty houses and quarrelsome performers, both in small, provincial theatres and the glamorous West End. And then, of course, had the unsurpassable thrill of a star being born and an unexpected hit.

A wonderful insight into the triumphs and disasters of the world of showbusiness from one of its leading figures.

Richard Stone was born in London and educated at Aldro School in Eastbourne and Charterhouse. After a short stint in his father's stockbroking business, he enrolled at RADA and was taken on as a student at Croydon Rep. He met his future wife, the actress Sara Gregory, when he was head-hunted by a Saltburn theatre-owner for the summer show. During the Second World War he served in the North Africa campaign, for which he was awarded the Military Cross and was wounded in action. His appointment as Entertainments Officer brought him back into showbusiness, and after the war he decided to continue putting on shows instead of returning to acting. He also became a theatrical agent, representing world-famous artistes, from Benny Hill to Victoria Wood.

Sadly, Richard died soon after publication of the hardback edition of his book in September 2000.

The author is donating all his royalties to Denville Hall and Brinsworth, the homes for actors and artistes.

YOU SHOULD HAVE BEEN IN *LAST* NIGHT

An Unusual Agent Remembers

Richard Stone

The Book Guild Ltd
Sussex, England

First published in Great Britain in 2000 by
The Book Guild Ltd
25 High Street
Lewes, East Sussex
BN7 2LU

Photo credits
Cover: Nobby Clarke (Dave Allen), Jeannie Savage/Telstar (Barbara Windsor),
Brian Moody (Victoria Wood), ©BBC 2000 (Bill Owen), Yorkshire TV (Bill Maynard).
Plate section: Syndication International (Saltburn Pier).

Extract Acknowledgments
Futura Publications for *Will the Real Ian Carmichael . . .* by
Ian Carmichael;Robson Books for *The Real Benny Hill* by Margaret Forwood;
The Stage Newspaper Ltd for the article reproduced on page 123.

Typesetting in Times by
IML Typographers, Chester, Cheshire

Printed in Great Britain by
Athenæum Press Ltd, Gateshead

A catalogue record for this book is available from
The British Library

ISBN 1 85776 602 4

This book is dedicated to my grandchildren Ben, Lara, Miranda, Nick and Rhett, all teenagers just starting out.

I hope that they all have good and fulfilling lives and experience as much love, happiness and fun as I have.

For those puzzled by my title I will explain. When an agent travels to Macclesfield to see his client in a play on a wet Wednesday in November and goes backstage after the performance, which was attended by 27 members of the public (19 of them with complimentary tickets), he is inevitably greeted with the words, 'You were a terrible audience; Monday and Tuesday it was packed. You should have been in *last* night.'

CONTENTS

FOREWORD

I first met Richard in the spring of 1976. I had left university in 1974, had won New Faces, been in a dire sketch show with Marti Caine and Lenny Henry for ATV, and had signed a personal management contract with an ex band leader in Hove without reading it. I had pretty much been out of work for two years when I decided it might be a good idea to get a proper agent. So I wrote to Roger Hancock, brother of the more famous Tony. He, unsurprisingly, wasn't keen to take on an unemployable singer songwriter with no act, and suggested I write to Richard Stone.

So I went to see Richard in his offices off the Strand, and he sat behind his desk, managing somehow to look affable and intimidating at the same time, and said 'Got good legs darling?'. Not the most politically correct question to ask a girl in the mid seventies, but Richard goes his own way, and I guess he needed someone for panto at Bromley. I don't have bad legs, as it happens, but a career as Dandini graduating to Aladdin wasn't exactly what I had in mind.

He suggested I go with the agency for a year, and if at the end of the year I hadn't earned £10,000 we would call it a day. Well, I didn't earn anything like that for years, but twenty years later I was still there.

Richard as an agent was a wonderful combination of being really sharp and on the ball when it came to doing deals, incredibly enthusiastic about show business, but never putting money over people, and never losing that feeling that at the end of the day, it wasn't worth upsetting people just to make a few more bob.

He was always supportive, and in a profession full of hard nosed sharks it was so lovely to be with someone so warm who never took it all too seriously.

Richard retired about ten years ago, and he's brilliant at it. He grows vegetables on his allotment on the Isle of Wight, he sails, he goes round the world on banana boats, he spends every summer entertaining all his different grandchildren. I try to go and see him and Sara with my children,

ix

and they pick raspberries and he takes them out in the dinghy and they love it.

Last autumn, I was sitting in my living room as the credits rolled on the first episode of 'Dinnerladies', when the phone rang. It was of course, Richard.

Victoria Wood

INTRODUCTION

When Benny Hill kept asking where I was, and Barbara Windsor missed me at the opening of her pantomimes (where's me fucking agent?) and Su Pollard left the office, all because I wasn't working full-time, I reckoned it was judicious to quit altogether. I would start a new phase of my life. And then I thought what a wonderful life I had been granted so far.

A happy childhood, a couple of years as a struggling actor, escaping death so often in the Second World War, and 50 fabulous years in show business looking after the likes of David Jason, Benny Hill, Dave Allen, Victoria Wood, Terry Scott, Bill Maynard and many others not so famous but good and funny friends nevertheless. When I used to entertain clients to dinner after their shows (a pleasant obligation for all agents) to divert them momentarily from listing their myriad worries, I would reminisce and tell stories of my life in show business.

The stories possibly were based on fact but over the years, and in my cups, may have become a trifle embroidered.

Possibly only to steer the conversation back to their problems several clients said at these dinners: 'You should write a book.'

So why not!
Sometime!

1

I get the showbusiness bug – watching pantomime, variety and a disastrous first night

My earliest memory is of visiting my maternal grandparents in Westbourne Grove, and of a magical contraption to fascinate a four-year-old. In truth it was only an outside larder with a rope and pulley worked like an old-fashioned lift. The groceries were piled in and I was allowed to pull on the rope propelling my treasure chest to the kitchen at the top of the five-storey house.

My other grandparents lived in Stroud, where I was sent when ill. Grandma Jane was an autocratic and imposing old lady, who happily took me on the local bus in the full throes of whooping cough. She had a glass eye, which frequently fell out when she bent over the coal bucket, whence I was ordered to retrieve it. When during the war my mother took the young and petite actress I was to marry to meet Grandma Jane, her imperious reaction was, 'Why does Dick intend to marry this schoolgirl?'

Grandpa Joe was a quiet man, who hid away in his greenhouse or with his collection of matchboxes.

When he was dying, Grandma Jane told my father that as usual Joe was pretending to be ill, so my parents took him back to their house, where he spent the last and probably most peaceful few days of his life.

My father, whom I adored, was a London stockbroker, dreaming of his retirement and returning to his beloved Cotswolds, where he was born. When he died we put on his tombstone simply the words 'A Cotswold Man'.

I was the first-born son to Jack and Maud Stone. Years later, when I was 14, mother confessed that she had once done something terrible and her elder son had to be told. It transpired that before she married father, when she was a VAD and he was on embarkation leave for Salonika, she gave herself to him, and there would have been a baby had she not miscarried. Tearfully she pleaded for my forgiveness, explaining that it had only happened because father was going almost certainly to his death on the

1

battle front. Even to a fairly unsophisticated schoolboy in the 1930s, her action seemed to be entirely defensible and I told her that she was not to worry any more on my account.

When I was three we moved from London to Sanderstead, then a small suburban village outside Croydon, and began to acquire the trappings of success. Our first motor car was an open Wolsey with a 'dickie' seat at the back. I occupied this seat with my teddy bear, which kept falling out onto the road, interrupting our outings to the country at a sedate 20 miles per hour.

My only brother Michael was born in 1926 and we moved to a larger house in Purley. Purley was posh, the Mecca for successful business types. Stockbrokers in top hats set off in convoy each morning at 8.10 a.m. like a fleet of penguins to walk to Purley Station for the 8.30 to London Bridge. Only if it poured with rain would my father, who was penny-wise, waste the penny ha'penny on the bus.

He'd get up early every morning to inspect his garden and pick a rose for his buttonhole. Arriving home at six, he went, in summer, to work in the vegetable garden or the greenhouse. In winter he went into his shed and built shelves and cupboards. He tried, in vain, to make me into a carpenter, keeping me for hours in the shed when I would so much rather have been listening to John Sharman's Music Hall on the wireless, with its improbably named stars, Stainless Stephen, Those Four Chaps, and Flotsam and Jetsam. Mr Murgatroyd and Mr Winterbotham, were actually Tommy Handley of ITMA fame, and Ronald Frankau, a sophisticated cabaret performer, one of whose songs included the statement:

'The preparatory school, the public school and the varsity
Produce a kind of fellow that is a scarcity'

How about that for political incorrectness? There was Mabel Constanduros with the Buggins Family, and most incongruous of all, the troupe of resident tap dancers, heard but not seen. There was also the unbelievably unfunny Norman Long – 'A song, a smile and a piano'. I remember one of his songs to this day. A certain store offered to lay linoleum free. His refrain ran:

Drages wonderful Drages
They always lay the lino on the floor.
Be it a mansion or be it a poor-house
They always lay the lino on the floor.

In those innocent days I'm convinced the plug was free.

Another of his presumably unsponsored songs was about the first Ford motors known as 'Tin Lizzies' until they went up-market.

2

No more squeaks and no more shakes
Now she's got those four-wheel brakes
Henry's made a lady out of Lizzie.

But in an era of utterly absurd and childish popular songs, this one about a bird takes the biscuit. Perpetrated I think by 'The Two Leslies' (Leslie Sarony and Leslie Holmes), the refrain ran

I lift up my finger and I say
Tweet tweet, shush shush, now now, come come

My love of show business had started early. Mother and I went to the Astoria, Purley, to see each new Fred Astaire and Ginger Rogers picture. Between films Robin Richmond, who later became one of radio's most famous organists, ascended as if by magic out of a deep pit in front of the screen, all the time playing the 'Mighty Compton Organ'. During this performance, the proscenium arch was a rainbow of light, continually changing colour. A penny ride from Purley was the Davis Theatre, Croydon. On Wednesday I maintain there was a matinee performance which offered two feature films, a 20-minute variety show, a free cup of tea and two biscuits for fourpence! My earliest visits to the theatre were to pantomime at the Grand, Croydon, where Sandy Powell ('Can you hear me, Mother?') always seemed to be playing Dame. Streatham Hill was the try-out theatre for London in those days and we would go *en famille* to see a show the week before it opened in the West End. One of my particular favourites was Leslie Henson (his son Nicky, whom I have represented since he left school, tells a tale that his father, who always played the Gaiety Theatre in the Aldwych, had a private line installed to the bar of the Waldorf Hotel next door, whence the call-boy would summon him for his next entrance). Leslie always had the same company, including Fred Emney and Richard Hearne. On the bill, in very small type, were his dance act, Cyril Richard and Madge Elliot, both later to become international stars.

Jack Hulbert and Cicely Courtneidge came to Streatham. In one of their shows, on its way to London, Cis sang a song with a line, 'Get up nice and early on the bus that leaves for Purley'. There was one small boy in the audience who was sure that she was singing it especially for him. Adoring both Jack and Cis, I was very pleased many years later, when Cis was in her eighties, and I was on the Awards Committee of the Variety Club of Great Britain, to suggest the inauguration of a Special Award for Services to Show Business – and successfully recommend Cicely Courtneidge.

Occasionally there was a week's variety at Streatham, topped by legendary names like Will Fyffe or Harry Lauder. But strangely enough, the one who sticks in my memory is Wilkie Bard, who must have been a very old man by this time, singing:

> I want to sing in opera
> I've got that kind of voice.
> I would have sung in opera
> If I had my choice.
> Signor Caruso (*Bom* on the drums)
> Told me I ought to do so.
> That's why I want to sing in opera
> Sing in op-op-op-era.

I wanted, desperately, to be at a first night in London. One of my favourite acts was the Houston Sisters. Renee Houston had gone solo and was opening in a revue at the London Hippodrome with George Robey, called *Certainly Sir*. Somehow mother wangled seats in the front row of the dress circle. The show was a disaster. George Robey had a line: 'This is my darkest hour.' The entire gallery shouted back, 'It certainly is!', and I still went into show business!

We had a billiard room but with no billiard table. It did, however, boast parquet flooring and a newfangled electric radiogram which played 10-inch records without having to be wound up by hand. The parquet floor and the radiogram were a great advantage, for we had one of the best locations in Purley for dances in the school holidays. We went from house to house for these dances, ice cream and jellies, and when in our teens, cider cup and our first dinner jackets, and always the same girls in long dresses smelling delicious and arousing our sensuality. Our discreet parents would look in from time to time. At worst they might have spotted a squeeze in a waltz, a cheek gently lowered, followed by a walk in the garden for a little petting.

At ten o'clock every morning the chauffeur drove my mother to the shops. In possibly the first Sainsbury's she would order this and that and it would be delivered by 12. I kept white mice which bred frequently. The same chauffeur would drive me to a pet shop in Croydon to sell the off-spring for tuppence each, keeping the expensive car tactfully out of sight of the shopkeeper.

I have a wandering eye and to this day strangers are not sure whether I am looking at them or someone over their shoulder. My parents spent a fortune trying to correct this, taking me twice a week in the holidays to a Miss Maddox in Welbeck Street for eye exercises. Through the left eye I peered into a binocular-type device and saw a lion and through the right eye a cage. To any normal-sighted person the result was that the lion was in the cage. I could never get the lion out of the forest, let alone into the cage!

4

My father hated going to the dentist, even though ours was a personal friend. If a tooth hurt he wasn't prepared to have it filled, it had to come out. He finally decided, whilst still in his forties, that he would have the lot, good and bad, removed and a false set installed.

Our earliest summer holidays were spent at Littlehampton, where Aunt Elsie and Uncle Will lived. Elsie was big and voluptuous and noisy, an off-stage pantomime principal boy. Uncle Will was kind and gave his five daughters sixpence a week pocket money; my father considered this out-rageous and not the way to teach children the value of money, so mine was set at threepence. Littlehampton was a village in the 1920s but did have a small wooden pavilion on the green where an unknown Elsie and Doris Waters sang genteel songs at the piano long before the days of Gert and Daisy.

But the best holidays were to come. For four years we went to Cadgwith, Cornwall. Cadgwith was beautiful and remote in the thirties – and wasn't the weather better in childhood! The greatest joy was getting to know my father and sharing his love of the outdoors. We went prawning with pointed nets chivvying the prawns from the seaweed and the over-hanging rocks. We would make a tripod with our nets, light a fire under-neath, with wood gathered from the beach and cook the prawns in sea water in a suspended biscuit tin. Or we'd set off, armed with pokers bent at the ends to form hooks for tickling lobsters out of deep crevices in the rocks. Or early in the morning, we would creep behind banks and hedges and, lying on our stomachs, wait for rabbits to shoot with a .22 rifle. Some of these simple pastimes have remained a joy to me all my life, and I loved my father for teaching them to me.

Foreign travel in those days was an event. One of my father's sisters, Dolly, had married one Henri Renauleaud, whom she had met whilst serv-ing in the Red Cross in France. He was general manager for Cognac Monet and so lived in Cognac. Mother and father were saying goodbye to Dolly and Henri on Victoria Station when my father suddenly decided I might benefit from a trip to France. As the *Golden Arrow* pulled out of the station there was an extra passenger with no luggage, no passport, just a note saying, 'I allow my brother-in-law, Henri Renauleaud, to take my son to Cognac, *Jack Stone*.' I was fitted out next day at a shop in Paris curiously called Little England with a change of clothing, and we contin-ued our journey to Cognac. What enchanted weeks in that glorious corner of France for a small boy, shopping with my aunt in the market, with the smell of fresh French bread, and watching the old men and boys with their long poles fishing in the slow-running Charente. Sitting on a stool in the sunshine by a French river under a parasol with a fishing line in the water, and only a minimal chance of a fish disturbing the peace, is more than a sport, it is a philosophy of life. I've loved the Charente ever since and visited my aunt each year until she died in her nineties in 1983.

My father's other sister, Jessie, was a beauty. She was famed for her 18-inch waist and her Victorian gowns. She was feather-brained and incongruously married at the time to Basil Liddell-Hart, probably the most influential military correspondent of his generation. It was said in the 1930s that if Liddell-Hart gave a bad notice in *The Times* to a military manoeuvre on Salisbury Plain, heads rolled. They lived in a flat in Baker Street, where Uncle Basil also had his office, where I was to be introduced to stars from another world, Bernard Shaw, Lawrence of Arabia, and J.B. Priestley. My aunt with her fabulous beauty charmed all these famous men, but eventually her sheer stupidity was too much for Basil. He divorced her and married his highly intelligent secretary, who, much to Jessie's chagrin, later became Lady Liddell-Hart.

We lived in Purley for all my formative years, seven to eighteen. It would be churlish and untrue to pretend that it was not a perfectly happy childhood, but I never liked Purley and all that it stood for. Perhaps it brought out the rebel in me. Before the age of 18 I had been a religious fanatic, a communist and finally an actor.

2

*At Aldro and Charterhouse, where the showbusiness bug
grows apace*

I was sent away to board at Aldro School in Eastbourne at eight years old,
and enjoyed most of it. It is arguable that sending mere infants away from
home so young is both lazy and barbaric. Nevertheless we sent both our
sons to Aldro. One loved it, one hated it. Jon Pertwee, who left after one
term, claimed always that it was for swinging in a Tarzan-like manner
from cistern to cistern on the lavatory chains that he was expelled. His
brother Michael, on the other hand, said their father Roland took him
away because he cried so much.

There were more schools in Eastbourne in the 1920s than days in the
year. My parents chose Aldro because they liked the look of Mrs Hill, the
headmaster's wife. She was indeed young and pretty with a sunny personality and made all the 60-odd young boys, banished from their homes, feel
that at least somebody loved them. Assistant masters at English preparatory schools are a weird bunch and Aldro was no exception. There was a
Major Someone, who walked with a stick, looked impressive, shouted a
lot and disappeared after a term or two under mysterious circumstances.
There was Miss Ward, who looked and behaved like Margaret Rutherford
and taught the juniors in a classroom away from the main building. She
seemed utterly unconnected with any other activity, as if she were running
a school of her own. And Miss Brown, the daughter of the first headmaster, a pretty, fading spinster who taught music and played the organ in
chapel. This organ had to be pumped by hand in a tiny cubicle at the back
of the chapel. It was an energetic task which seemed somehow to be allotted to me too often. It was easy to doze off during a hymn when the organ
would cease to function and dying groans of 'Fast fall the eventide' would
summon me quickly back to frenzied and rather too noisy pumping.

The master loved and remembered by us all was H.B. Craft. The son of
a moderate painter whom we boys were taught to believe was on a par
with Michelangelo, Mr Craft was physically an unattractive man with a

badly assembled face and an apology of a nose upon which rested, rather precariously, steel-rimmed spectacles. He had an atrocious and wobbly tenor voice and in every school concert would sing innumerable songs right off-key.

Mr Craft gave his life, every moment of it, to Aldro and its pupils. In his desk he had a ruler and bars of chocolate. You had to be very wicked or lazy to get the gentlest rap on the knuckles with the ruler. You only had to keep awake and not be totally obtuse to be rewarded in almost every class with a piece of chocolate. He lived around the corner from the school in a one-roomed flat above a shop in Meads Village. Every Sunday, eight or nine boys would be invited for a sumptuous tea. He must have spent all his meagre salary on us boys. In the Christmas holidays he took a party of older boys and their sisters skiing. The parents were charged a ridiculously small amount which barely covered the cost and once more he came up with 'treats'. He bought us coffee and delicious cakes and hired us fancy dress for the dances. I was given, and still have, a silver cigarette case, inscribed, 'For the boy who made the most skiing progress, Wengen 1932' – not the best, mind you, just the one who made most progress! H.B. Craft never appeared without his camera. His Christmas cards, which were sent out on a mammoth distribution list, were montages of the previous year's activities at Aldro, ranging from a group of the first cricket eleven to a close-up of Matron. In later years he invited old boys to his annual lunch; the generosity of the man knew no bounds.

Dominating this little scholastic empire was another remarkable man, F.E. Hill, the headmaster and owner of the school, then in his thirties. With curly, black hair, athletic and good-looking, he had a wild, almost satanic look. He was probably difficult to live with, and maybe sank a drop or two behind the baize door which separated the school proper from the private quarters. Years later there were ugly rumours circulating among the old boys of goings-on with the matron. But he was a great schoolmaster and taught us all never-to-be-forgotten standards of behaviour, in the most rigorous surroundings. He was a lay preacher and personally conducted services in chapel every morning and twice on Sunday. He frightened me with his fanatical religious zeal, until at some incongruous misdemeanour by a small boy his stern face would break into a warm smile.

In winter it was so cold in the dormitories that for the morning wash one had to break the ice in the bedside jug of water. Summer and winter, the day at Aldro began by all the boys swimming two lengths of the unheated swimming pool, and first to plunge in was the headmaster. Our rugby field was on Beachy Head. After running a mile up hill you came upon a dip in the Downs where the rugger field was perched, so near to the cliff edge that a good long kick could send a ball into the sea! It was cold and windy in shorts on Beachy Head in March. I had chillblains on my fingers so big

8

that they burst. Sports day took place on the cricket field, with our parents ensconced on a bank above, looking down on the activities. At the end of the day there was a drill display. It was in the days when Britain still had an Empire and we were divided into squads, India, South Africa, Australia, New Zealand, Canada and West Indies. To the tune of 'Colonel Bogey' played on a portable gramophone, perched on an upturned biscuit tin to increase the resonance, the six squads formed the spokes of a revolving cartwheel. When Mr Craft blew his whistle we turned outwards and marched towards the edge of the field; when Mr Craft blew his whistle again we should have turned back, but I didn't hear the whistle and resolutely led my gang up the bank into the ranks of the astonished parents.

This sports day was on the Saturday of half-term. We were not allowed home so my parents stayed the weekend in the Cavendish Hotel. We were allowed out to breakfast on Sunday, and then came back with our parents to chapel. One Sunday I ate too much and, to my parents' utter shame, I returned the full English breakfast down the aisle.

There were small strips of garden, and those interested could have one to cultivate flowers, lettuces and radishes – anything, in fact, which would grow to maturity in the space of a ten-week term. Those boys who liked weeding or were sufficiently sycophantic could also volunteer to help in Mr Hill's private garden at weekends. A list of such keen gardeners was posted on the notice board. I cultivated yet another plot. In the drawer of my washstand I planted mustard and cress on a damp towel. It was growing well. Sadly Crispin, F.E. Hill's six-year-old son, playing in the dormitories whilst we were out, discovered my secret. Joyously he brought along matron to have a look. Sternly she brought along the headmaster. Mr Hill's only reaction was to write against my name on the list of keen gardeners – 'too keen'.

Boys gathered for each new term at Victoria Station to join the school special for Eastbourne. Our trunks and tuck boxes contained jam and cakes which supplemented our spartan evening meals. We were allowed to bring ten shillings for pocket money. This was handed in on arrival and we were issued a miniature chequebook. After lunch on Sunday bottles of disgusting sticky sweets were produced and we bought our ration with a cheque. On Saturday nights, we had magic lantern lectures. One lecturer sticks in my mind as he had the remarkable name of Septimus Pears. He had a billiard cue which he banged on the floor for the next slide; we applauded and giggled if the slides came up in the wrong order, or best of all upside down. If the lecturer failed to turn up Mr Craft sang!

The big 'treat' was on Ascension Day. In a hired South Down coach we were taken to the Long Man of Wilmington, a huge chalk figure on a slope of the South Downs, the exact origin of which remains a mystery. We, however, were more interested in rolling down from top to bottom! We walked then to Alfriston clutching sixpence to spend in the village shop. The day finished with a slap-up tea at Drusillas. In my first ever photo album there is a small sepia snapshot. It depicts only a stretch of rolling Downs and sky and underneath, in schoolboy handwriting is the curious caption: *Ascension Day 1930.*

At Aldro my nick name was Christopher, for the one and only disc jockey of the day was Christopher Stone, who, if my memory is not at fault, actually put the records onto the turntable himself and probably wound up the gramophone! The name was to haunt me later. Sara and I frequently dined a few years ago at a delightful hotel-restaurant – Peacock Vane. Drinks were served in the drawing room from the piano top and the proprietress, a Mrs Joan Wolfenden, presided over the proceedings while at the same time busying herself with her embroidery. She always welcomed me as Christopher, and once went so far as to recall that when she was a schoolgirl she had first met me at the BBC with Elsie and Doris Waters. I hesitated to tell her that if indeed I was Christopher Stone, I must be a very sprightly old man of well over 90!

If F.E. Hill had not been a schoolmaster, he would have been an actor. He loved 'theatricals'. In the 1930s, Clarkson Rose played every summer with his famous concert party, Twinkle, on the pier at Eastbourne. There was an annual cricket match between Aldro and Twinkle. Clarkie's team consisting not only of himself and his supporting cast but also the rose-buds – the six genteel young ladies selected by Clarkie and his wife Olive Fox as chorus. My father, I remember, heartily disapproved of his son playing cricket with 'rogues and vagabonds'. Maybe he had an idea of the way my inclinations would lead me, and hated the thought even then that I would not carry on in his image, and might finish up 'poofing about in some tatty show on the end of a pier'. Strangely enough, I nearly did – and in Twinkle!

A special feature of Clarkie's show were the spangled curtains, or 'tabs', on which were emblazoned in silver glitter the word 'Twinkle'. When Clarkie died he was cremated at Eastbourne. We were a small gathering at the crematorium and as his coffin disappeared on the rollers, a dingy pair of faded brown curtains was drawn on his last exit. An elderly comedian sitting beside me said with some regret, 'Oh dear, Clarkie wouldn't have liked those tabs.'

In the 60s, I presented shows myself in Eastbourne. The day after one disastrous opening night, the entertainments chief for the corporation, an Eastbourne establishment figure named George Hill, phoned me in my London office. After justifiably criticising the entire shambles, he picked on the leading comedian: 'Richard, some of his jokes were in very poor taste. The man is a bounder. I don't know how you allowed him to appear, and you with the benefit of an education at Aldro.'

10

My final memory of Aldro is perhaps the most important. Mr Hill was a prominent member of the Eastbourne Amateur Dramatic Society. During one term-time the current production was a thriller *The Crooked Billet*. Mr Hill was the villainous innkeeper and his unwitting assistant was Alf the pot boy. He suggested that I should play Alf, and I was nightly abducted by my own headmaster from the dormitory after lights out. We drove to the Devonshire Park Theatre for rehearsals and, subsequently, for the performances. Thank you, F.E. Hill, for awakening in a small boy a yearning for the 'smell of the greasepaint'. Thank you for giving me, so young, the key that later opened the door to a life in the most exciting profession in the world.

I moved on from Aldro to Charterhouse, whose main buildings are perched gracefully on a hill in rural Surrey, looking down on the small town of Godalming. My house, Lockites, however, was built in a hole with windows that faced a dripping-wet bank. Inside were stone steps worn away by generations of schoolboys, flanked by iron railings like prison bars; outside lavs were primitive. To reach the main building you climbed, several times a day, 42 'Lockite' steps.

The sleeping quarters were wooden cubicles open at the top, so that by standing on the bed, 'tossing off' could be enjoyed with your friend in the next cubicle. It's not surprising really that a lot of this went on, when you consider that young developing males of 13 to 17 years old were deprived of female company. It had no effect on future life as all the participants are now married and pillars of society, except one poor sod who was caught and expelled. I see him sometimes on the beach with his grandchildren, but I don't mention the 'good old days'.

Lockites was a hideous and uncomfortable building which has now been replaced in a pleasant location with a modern centrally heated 'Hilton' and girls!

Being an atrocious games player, I was an outsider. At soccer I never progressed beyond a team appropriately, if insultingly, called Etceteras. I took advantage of any activity which allowed me to escape games. The most bizarre was keeping ferrets. Ferrets are vicious little animals which bite at every opportunity. I was permitted to keep them in the yard of the laundry, well away from human habitation. Ferreting involves small round nets being placed over one end of a rabbit warren. The ferret is then sent in at the other end and hopefully the rabbit flees for his life into the net. If the ferret catches the rabbit, it gorges itself and then goes to sleep in the warren. This entails a long and patient vigil by the owner, if the ferret is not to be lost. There was a suitable bank with rabbit warrens near the headmaster's house. It was a lonely occupation and my only companion was, curiously enough, the distinguished headmaster himself, Sir Frank Fletcher, who appeared to enjoy my antics.

11

I was in the choir, not because I was an embryo Pavarotti, but because I was one of the few who volunteered.

To be 'in bounds' at Charterhouse, it was not permitted to cross any of the railway lines which neatly encircled the school, putting towns of any size, including Godalming, Guildford and Aldershot, 'out of bounds'. Godalming and Guildford had no particular attraction for me but Aldershot had a second-rate music hall playing weekly variety shows and touring revues. I acquired a motorbike, which I secreted in a garage near the school. On Saturday nights, heavily disguised, I would drive to the first house at the Aldershot Hippodrome. I was fairly sure of not being caught as Charterhouse masters were rarely, if ever, in the audience, unable to appreciate my delight at seeing Clapham and Dwyer, Johnson Clark, 'The Sportsman Ventriloquist', Leonard Henry and Jack Hylton's Band.

My form master at the time of sitting for School Certificate was W.C. Sellars. This amusing man had written, with an Eton schoolmaster, one Yeatman, the hilarious *1066 and All That*. It was a bestseller and later became a twice-revived, successful, musical revue in London. Sellars brought his humour into the classroom, especially in history lessons. I worshipped the man and his manner. My history essay for the exam was frivolous, and written in the style of 'the master', but I got my credit.

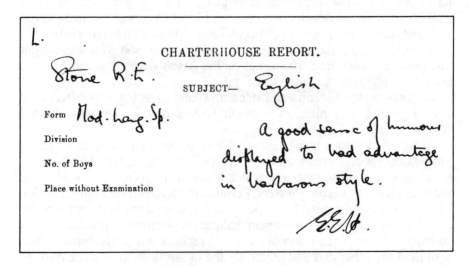

L.

CHARTERHOUSE REPORT.

Stone R.E.

SUBJECT— English

Form Mod. Lang. Sp.

Division

No. of Boys

Place without Examination

a good sense of humour displayed to bad advantage in barbarous style.

E.E.A.

Lockites had a very active dramatic society. Our house tutor, W.O. Dickens (The WOD) encouraged us with play readings on Sunday in his delightful house. One year we presented a mixed bag of entertainment including a one-act play, *The Stoker*, in which I played the title role. My leading lady was Patrick Shovelton, then a weedy lad with chronic asthma who was taken ill at the last moment. He was replaced by W.O. Dickens' young bride, Mary, a beautiful girl in her early twenties. Discovering a few years ago that the Dickens had retired to a village near us, I called in and told a surprised Mary Dickens that I had been in love with her for 50 years!

When I became a member of the Charterhouse Dramatic Society I began to enjoy my life at school. The Crazy Gang were currently performing at the London Palladium in *All Alight at Oxford Circus*. We presented *All Alight at Scholars Court*, a revue devised and produced by Ronald Millar and Richard Stone, sketches and lyrics by Richard Stone, music by Ronald Millar, general manager, Ian Wallace. Ronnie, later Sir Ronald Millar, was a successful author of plays in his own right. He adapted for the theatre most of the C.P. Snow novels, and was on the board of the Haymarket Theatre Group. Despite all this, I am told he was knighted for his contribution to Maggie Thatcher's speeches! Ronnie was an indifferent actor for a short time during the war, after being invalided out of the Navy. He played some leading roles in the West End, thanks to the wartime scarcity of young actors. At school my opinion of his acting was shared by one who has remained a lifelong friend, the singer, actor and TV personality, Ian Wallace. Ian and I agreed that the one thing that must not happen in the revue was for Ronnie to act and sing. We tactfully persuaded him that by far the most distinguished role for him as a performer was to conduct his own music with the Charterhouse Dance Band. This he did at the age of 17 in white tie and tails and white gloves!

Charterhouse has a strong theatrical tradition. From our time, not only Ian, Ronnie and I, but several others were in 'the profession'. In a sketch which I wrote and played in called 'The Matron', a mother was asking inane questions of the matron, and one Peter Dunlop played the mother. Peter also became a theatrical agent, and his distinguished clients, like mine, would perhaps have been surprised to catch him in female attire.

For some obscure reason, the terms at Charterhouse are called 'quarters' despite the fact that there are only three. To make matters even worse the winter term is called the 'Oration Quarter'. We produced *All Alight at Scholars Court* in the Oration Quarter 1936. Having reserved for myself the star spot at the end of the show, I gave impersonations of several masters, including the headmaster. This and other irreverencies proved too much for Sir Frank Fletcher, who in his end of quarter address to the school said of our revue: 'It was excellent but must never happen again.'

My final memory of Charterhouse is of Alf Tressler, who was one of the greatest schoolmasters of his era. He taught the sixth form modern language specialists, of which I was one. His boundless enthusiasm for Goethe, Racine, Corneille, Molière and Anatole France could not fail to arouse in any sensitive boy a love of these great classics. His catchphrase, 'You may take notes, it is not forbidden', was echoed in chorus by his pupils. Above his desk was a wicked caricature of Alf captioned with these same words. In his end of quarter report on a particularly bad class, he wrote of the boy who came second, 'In the Kingdom of the Blind, the one-eyed is King. Hence his position of Viceroy'. Of me he once wrote, 'He shows interest in his work, but his observations are not always relevant or discreet.' Outside the classroom he was a friendly man who lived with his sister half a mile from the school. Most of the year he could be seen in khaki shorts and a panama hat, tending his garden or, with a curious veil attached to a boater, fearlessly extracting the honey from his beehives.

I left Charterhouse in the summer of 1937 and joined Alf on his annual cycling expedition to the Continent with a party of boys, including Patrick Shovelton. We cycled hard and boys were frequently left behind with the vaguest instruction as to where Alf possibly intended to stay the night. Poor Patrick Shovelton had an attack of asthma and was left in hospital in Brussels, and later transferred to a hospital in Bopart with pleurisy, being told to return home as best he could when recovered. I sat next to Pat at a Charterhouse Founders Day dinner in 1999. He has recovered and in his eighties can still play 36 holes of golf a day! We cycled round the beautiful, tiny, hilly country of Luxembourg, and finally reached the Rhine. In Germany we stayed in Hitler Youth hostels. In Bacharach, we were inspected by Rudolf Hess, at that time the head of the Hitler Youth movement. I have found some letters I wrote to my parents at this most interesting of times in Germany just before World War II. I quote:

At Deutsche Ringendherberge Bacharach —

> I have just had a look round the room and on the wall is a list of the jews who have shops in this village. Underneath is written 'who buys from these shops is a traitor to his people'.

And later I wrote:

> Outside nearly every German village there are notices saying, 'JEWS NOT WANTED HERE' 'ARYAN MARRIED WOMEN AND GIRLS BEWARE OF THE JEWS, THEY ARE YOUR DOWNFALL' 'NO PARKING FOR JEWS HERE'.

I remember long evening discussions with Alf Tressler on this trip about my own future. My father desperately wanted me to join him on the Stock Exchange and to prepare me to eventually take over his flourishing business. I wanted, equally desperately, to be an actor. Alf knew this but wisely told me I should join my father.

14

With my whole life before me, this at least would prove to my father a willingness to satisfy his dream. Undoubtedly Alf guessed that it would only be for a few months, and so it turned out.

3

RADA, the Saltburn show — and meeting Sara

During the autumn of 1937 I commuted, with my father, from Purley to the City and tried hard to enjoy life as an office boy in his stockbroking firm. I duly stuck on stamps and ran errands whilst the staff tried hard to pretend that the new office boy was not the senior partner's son.

It was at a cocktail party in Purley that I confided to a middle-aged fellow guest, himself in a vocational profession, my burning desire to become an actor. He made a point of finding my father and introducing himself. He must have proved very persuasive for, on the way home in the car, the delicate subject of my future was broached. Father could never understand why I could be so foolish as to want to turn down a ready-made and secure career for something as risky as the theatre. And far worse, he was convinced that all actors were 'pansies and lounge lizards'. He must have now felt that he was fighting a losing battle, for he reluctantly agreed to send me to drama school.

In the spring of 1938, after a cursory entrance exam and an interview with the principal, Kenneth Barnes, I was enrolled at the Royal Academy of Dramatic Art. Father took a long time to accept my new life, and for nearly two years we barely spoke. Apart from the strain of life at home, my time at the RADA was sheer joy. Before the war there were only a handful of drama schools, and a severe shortage of male students!

I'm not convinced that dramatic training is any more valuable to an actor than practical experience. Amongst the stars of my era who never went to drama school are Rex Harrison, Margaret Rutherford and Irene Handl. Charles Laughton was sent away, considered to be without talent. Today pop stars, boxers and TV personalities become actors and get away with it. I personally learnt more by working in the holidays than during the term at RADA. Managing to get taken on as a student at the famous Croydon Rep, I had the privilege of working under Michael Barry, later to become Head of Drama at the BBC. The company included Richard Wattis, who after the war played always the vacuous English upper-class idiot in dozens of comedy films, and Dennis Price, who to my mind was

16

the best ever Jeeves to Ian Carmichael's Bertie Wooster on TV. A fellow student/ASM was Edna Doré, who came into her own in her seventies playing assorted grandmothers and other geriatric ladies, at the National, on TV and in films.

The Christmas production in 1938 was *1066 and All That* by my form teacher, W.C. Sellars. Engaged as student assistant stage manager and general understudy at one pound a week, my role included opening and closing by hand the curtains (known as No. 1 runners) on each scene. Richard Wattis would then saunter on in front with a long cigarette holder and introduce the next historical event which was being set up behind. Unfortunately, on his first entrance on the opening night, I pulled over-enthusiastically and enveloped the urbane Richard in a set of curtains. The next night, my reputation was restored when a dear actor, Stafford Byrne, playing the central character of the Common Man was taken ill. I took over his enormous role at very short notice indeed and received my first review in a professional company. The *Croydon Times* headed their column, 'Purley actor steps into the breach'. It was fortunate that the local critic had not attended the first night.

The ratio of four girls to one man at RADA had its advantages. I was able to choose as my girlfriend a humorous and beautiful blonde, Diana Marshall. I was still a virgin at the time and, despite my determined efforts, Diana was not prepared to come to bed. My chum at RADA was John Barron. John at that time was a shy, handsome, slightly freckled-faced, red-headed boy. He has now made his reputation portraying establishment figures in his various roles as bishop, lawyer and business tycoon. A far cry this from the youth sitting on Purley Station, waiting to be collected by me for a weekend visit and avidly recording the numbers of passing trains!

In the spring of 1939 an extraordinary lady visited RADA with an equally extraordinary mission. Mrs Miriam Osborne owned a café and a small theatre in the tiny Yorkshire seaside town of Saltburn. For many years, in association with the singer Harry Tollfree, she had presented a show under the misleading title *The Little Theatre Cabaret*. It had been a conventional nine-handed concert party of the type that in pre-war days could be found in the smallest seaside resort. Saltburn was a very small resort indeed and could not attract a high standard of concert party artiste.

Whilst Tommy Trinder was in Sandown, Clarkson Rose in Eastbourne, Arthur Askey in Shanklin, and the brilliant Fol-de-Rols in Scarborough, Bournemouth or Torquay, Saltburn got Harry Tollfree and his partner Doris Yorke singing duets with all the confidence but not the skill of Anne Ziegler and Webster Booth. Miriam Osborne decided to start again, except for Harry Tollfree, with youngsters who would make up in youthful enthusiasm what they lacked in experience. She came to RADA on a search.

She saw me as the stage manager in Thornton Wilder's wonderful play *Our Town* and asked if I would like to join her troupe. Could I write some sketches, could I present a different seven-minute act for each of the six programmes? I hesitated only momentarily before saying yes on both counts. Mrs Osborne then said that I would need to supply my own modern wardrobe, a dinner jacket for the opening and tails for the finale. Rehearsals were not paid for and my salary would be £4 10s a week starting on the opening night, 1st July. I wanted the job badly but still had the temerity to ask if Diana could be included as comedienne to work with me in the sketches. Diana was interviewed and engaged at £3 10s. We were both only halfway through our RADA training and so had to leave before the summer. Sir Kenneth Barnes was horrified, not only that we were not going to complete the course, but that we were going into vaudeville – and at Saltburn! Two other RADA students, not known to us, were engaged but they at least had completed their training.

Tom Hammerton was a friend of Mrs Osborne and had been instrumental in bringing her to the RADA. He also asked for his girlfriend, Sara Gregory, to be included in the cast. There were several weeks now to fill in before the summer, and so I started the hard trek around the agents. There was the formidable Miriam Warner, who booked anyone anywhere and whose opening line, if you eventually got past the receptionist, was 'Do you speak lines, dear?' There was Robert Layton, who specialised in concert party artistes and had a map of England on his wall. On the map the coastline was dotted with flags of different colours indicating the towns in which he had booked comedians, comediennes, light comedians, dancing juveniles, baritones, tenors, sopranos, soubrettes, pianists and speciality acts. Above his office in Cambridge Circus were two young agents starting in business under the name of G.W. Direction. The partners of G.W. Direction were Derek Glynne and Felix De Wolfe. They were 'legit' agents, a curious distinctive title given to anyone from manager to actor in the straight theatre – as opposed to variety. Felix de Wolfe fixed me a 'special week' at the Theatre Royal, Brighton, in *Jane Eyre* at a salary of 30 shillings including rehearsals; I played the old clergyman who marries Rochester and Jane. Felix came down to see the performance, not on the strength of my three shillings commission but to see the artistes he had booked to play Jane Eyre and Rochester. Determined to impress with my five-line part as an old man, I was covered in applied wrinkles and shaking with assumed senility. An old lady in the next seat and obviously short-sighted, turned to Felix and said, 'Oh dear, they should really let that poor old man retire.' Felix apparently thought it was more appropriate to let that young actor retire.

Despite his opinion, I was re-engaged by J. Baxter Somerville for a six-week season in his Regency Players at Huddersfield, at £3 a week. I was to 'play as directed', but following my debut at Brighton, Baxter Somerville had cast me in a selection of elderly character parts. Unfortunately I was 19 and the other 'elderly character' actor was 70. The incongruity of our teaming as the two old uncles in *Whiteoaks* was too much for our director, Richard Wattis, and I was sacked after one week. This was a shock not only to my pride but to my sex life. I was sharing digs with a young actress whose name ashamedly now escapes me. We'd got as far as 'heavy petting' but, thinking that we had plenty of time ahead, I still hadn't lost my virginity, when I was summarily and instantly dismissed. Casual one-night stands were not yet the fashion; maybe I should have been born a generation later!

The next few weeks were spent planning the summer show. We met the three other members of the troupe, and our pianist Julian Oakley. There were tremendous battles over the choice of material between us young-sters and Harry. We wanted an original revue, Harry knew that seaside audiences expected 'corn'. A compromise was reached: we included sketches which I was to write, and some original songs by Julian Oakley and myself, together with much 'tried and true' concert party material.

Today, with television devouring scripts at a rate of knots, comedy writ-ing is a highly skilled and competitive business. In a different world two old gentlemen called Rutherford and Wilcock supplied the season's rights to perform their ghastly numbers for two or even three guineas, depending on the stature of the concert party.

It was on the 'train call' to Saltburn that I fell in love with the girl who was to become my lover, my wife, the mother of my three children, my partner, my best friend and my constant support for the next 60-odd years and, God willing, for a little while yet. Sara Gregory was born in Sydney and brought up in Adelaide. Her parents were English but she was, techni-cally, Australian. Determined to become an actress, she left Australia at the age of 17 to come 'home', hopefully to train at RADA and make her name in London. She had succeeded so far, winning at RADA not only the Bronze Medal at the annual public show, but the Athene Seyler award for comedy. It was also fairly indicative of her determination that, still only 18, in the Christmas holidays from RADA she attended an 'open' audition for the chorus of a small provincial pantomime, and was given instead the title role of Cinderella. This she had played three times daily for a week each in, of all salubrious dates, Scunthorpe, Grimsby, Bishop Auckland and Oldham. She was, and still is, petite, beautiful, kind, generous and totally without malice.

Our digs in Saltburn which were to be our home for the next 14 weeks had been fixed by Mrs Osborne. To prevent 'goings-on' she split the couples, so Sara and I were booked into Ruby House, Ruby Street. It all began on the very first night when we arrived and Sara asked me to her

THE LITTLE THEATRE

SALTBURN-BY-THE-SEA

Lessee: M. O. OSBORNE.

THE LITTLE THEATRE CABARET

NINTH SEASON
(under the direction of Harry Tollfree)

TOM HAMMERTON

SARA GREGORY

RICHARD STONE

DIANA MARSHALL

JULIAN OAKLEY

HILDA JACKSON

TOM KENNEDY

BETTY GLOVER

HARRY TOLLFREE

2/-, 1/6, 1/-, (including tax)

Booking Office: SALTBURN CAFE, LTD.   Tel.: SALTBURN 103.

All Seats Bookable.   No Extra Charge.

The Saltburn Cafe Car Park is free to the Patrons of this Theatre

20

room, claiming that she could not open the clasp of her trunk. At last I lost my virginity.

In 1999 Sara and I spent a weekend with Ian Carmichael at his lovely Yorkshire home. He drove us the odd 15 miles to Saltburn for a nostalgic visit. Sadly our theatre is now an amusement arcade, but we found Ruby House, now three separate flats. On the first floor flat we found our bedroom where it all started and the front room where late into the night I wrote all those songs and sketches for programmes 2 to 6.

The show in Saltburn was hard work. We changed the programme every three days so that all six programmes were produced in the space of two weeks' rehearsal and the first three weeks of performing. We rehearsed all day and did the show in the evening. By now Harry seemed to have conceded that the *Little Theatre Cabaret 1939* could be mostly original material and there was a lot to be written. Apart from Sara and Diana there were two other girls in the company. One was a genteel young friend of Mrs Osborne's, of limited ability, the other was Betty Glover, a girl of some talent. Betty played the piano tolerably well, and she and I worked up six double acts of supposedly sophisticated comedy material, one of which featured in each programme.

The Little Theatre, Saltburn, was a hut on the blunt end of one of the smallest piers in England. The stage and dressing rooms were so small that from the back wall of the 'theatre' to the footlights was about 15 foot. On the right of the stage was a small room where the four girls changed their costumes and on the left a similar room for the men. There was no passing backstage – there was no backstage! The girls came on from the right and the men from the left. The pianist sat on stage at the piano and stayed there all evening. Of the three shows in town, we were still considered to have the number one pitch. Beryl Reid, appearing as soubrette in the *Arcadian Follies* in the town hall, told me that she considered us being in a different league. Perhaps she was unhappy with her billing, which was very small indeed! The star of the *Arcadian Follies* was a comedian billed in large type as 'GEORGE S. YOUNG, who has appeared before all the crowned heads of Europe, including Prince Chichi-Bou of China'.

En route from our digs in Ruby Street there was a winding cliff path and below us the pitch of the alfresco troupe 'Ma Grapho's Follies' on the sands. Open-air shows clearly could not charge admission and collected their earnings by 'bottling'. This ancient custom required the artistes themselves to go round the sparse audience with jam jars, making a collection. Sadly, cunning holidaymakers, and especially children, knew when they had seen enough and beat a hasty retreat to avoid paying. It was the custom to allow each member of the company a benefit night, when he or she would be given the entire collection. A wintertime fisherman rechristened for the season, 'La Tagata, the famous Italian tenor', seemed out of luck. For a whole week it rained. Daily, as we made our way to the Little Theatre, came an announcement from the beach: 'Ladies and gentlemen, due to today's inclement weather, once again we are happy to announce that tomorrow's performance will be La Tagata's benefit night.'

There was an elderly sister act, one of whom, I swear, had a wooden leg, which she managed to keep off stage on their tented platform, whilst tap dancing with the other!! I found out some 20 years into representing the Yorkshire comedian Joe Black that he had been the juvenile in 'Ma Grapho's Follies'.

We did above average business and broadcast weekly on the North Regional programme, *Round the Shows*, one of our excerpts being picked up nationally. I shall never forget the thrill of receiving a telegram from Robert Layton, the agent, telling me that Clarkson Rose, no less, had heard a broadcast by Richard Stone and Betty Glover 'The BBC's new comedy duo' and wished to audition us when our season finished, with a view to us joining Twinkle for the 1940 season!

War was declared at the beginning of September. I went, by train, to Middlesbrough and enlisted as a gunner. At 19 I was too young and was to wait six months for my call-up. The Little Theatre had a glass roof and if we were to complete the last two weeks of our season to comply with the blackout regulations, it had to be painted. We did it ourselves, but the fun had gone, and so had the audiences.

I was 19 at Saltburn, really in love for the first time, and blissfully happy, starting out on a career which had been inevitable since Alf the pot-boy seven years before. How could we stage-struck band of young vagabonds have known then that, for the next six years, the shores of England would resound to the booming of an ever-growing army of anti-aircraft guns where once had boomed the baritone voices of a multitude of Harry Tollfrees?

22

4

A chilly experience with Sea Breezes, *an outing with Derek Farr, and getting married*

In 1939 I was given another six months' grace before joining the army. I went back to Purley, Sara stayed with her uncle and aunt in London. Our sex life was helped along by another of Sara's army of old aunts who turned a blind eye to what went on in her studio. Mary McLeod, known as Dolly, a distinguished artist then in her seventies, was the eldest. She lived in a ground floor studio at 17A Gerald Road. It was a romantic abode, despite its approach through a long dark passage beside the police station. Her bedroom clung like a Swiss chalet halfway up the wall, with slatted wooden windows opening onto the main living area below. Above her lived Noël Coward. We spent many happy hours there and often heard 'the master' composing above. Noël seriously wanted to add Dolly's rented studio to his own and went to great lengths to acquire the lease from their joint landlord. After the war, when Dolly was 80 and dead broke, he discovered that she was unable to pay the rent and stopped trying to get her out. He paid her rent until the day she died.

One activity at this time was taking part in troop shows organised by Felix De Wolfe from the Arts Theatre Club. I believe the picture showing me as a fairy queen was taken at the RAF station at Biggin Hill.

On declaration of war London West End theatres were closed. With the boundless enthusiasm of youth, and convinced that our Saltburn show should be seen by a wider audience, I became an impresario and began the round of agents to see if we could beg, borrow or rent a theatre or hall in the suburbs. Jack Olliphant, a small-time agent, found us a hall in Southgate, North London. With incredible optimism, we decided that like the famous Windmill, we would play continuously from 1 p.m. daily. It is doubtful if Southgate then or now could support a one-night visit of a major star, let alone an open-ended season of continuous performances by a bunch of unknowns. We called the show *Sea Breezes* and pushed hundreds of leaflets announcing our arrival through the letter boxes of the

A Show you must not miss!

SPRINGFIELD HALL

SPRINGFIELD ROAD (5 minutes walk from Arnos Grove tube station)

At Last A First Class LIVE SHOW for SOUTHGATE

OPENING DATE

Saturday, October 7th

TWICE DAILY

The first London Presentation of the North of England's Most Famous

B.B.C. CONCERT PARTY

'SEA BREEZES'

Produced by Harry Tollfree and Richard Stone

RICHARD STONE & BETTY GLOVER THE B.B.C. CRAZY ACT	SARA GREGORY ROYAL COMMAND PERFORMER THE POPULAR PERSONALITY SINGER

CAROL RAYE	THE BEAUTIFUL AND TALENTED STAR FROM BOBBY HOWE'S "BOBBY GET YOUR GUN"

HARRY TOLLFREE THE YORKSHIRE STAR BARITONE	GORDON HUMPHRIS JESSIE MATTHEW'S DANCING PARTNER IN THE FILM "I CAN TAKE IT"

GUEST ARTISTES	WILL BE INTRODUCED FROM TIME TO TIME

ROY ELLIS Ace Television Pianist	HILDA JACKSON ═══ IMPRESSIONIST

FORGET THE WAR FOR TWO HOURS IN THE COMPANY OF THESE BRILLIANT ENTERTAINERS WHOM HARRY S. PEPPER INTRODUCED ON THE RADIO RECENTLY IN HIS BROADCASTING TOUR OF SEASIDE RESORTS

AFTERNOONS at 3 o'clock   NIGHTLY at 7.30

☞ *Watch for the announcement of our local* ☜
AMATEUR TALENT COMPETITION

Admission: Afternoons 6d. & 1/- Evenings 9d., 1/-, 1/6

uninterested residents of Southgate. The leaflets, known as 'throwaways', have never been more appropriately named, for when we arrived at Southgate to rehearse for our grand opening night, it was discovered that the hall secured by Jack Olliphant was not licensed for music and dancing. The Windmill never closed, we never opened.

Sara's formidable Uncle Lance, who by now had taken an active dislike to me, phoned Purley to pour scorn on the fiasco and to deplore Sara's involvement with *Sea Breezes* and me. Father answered the phone. He must have thought that I had shown some initiative, for with well-worn truisms, such as 'kicking a man when he was down', he burnt up the line to Prince Albert Mansions. It was the beginning of a new understanding with my father.

He helped to finance, with Felix De Wolfe and Derek Glynne, a transfer of *Sea Breezes*, retitled *The Black Knights*, to the Purley Hall, where we played more realistically one show a night for quite a success-ful six-week season. By now we had been joined by Leslie Julian-Jones, a brilliant pianist, composer and lyric writer and future leading light in that now defunct, but then integral part of London theatre, the intimate revue. During the run of *The Black Knights* I went to East-bourne with Betty Glover, to audition for Clarkson Rose in the deserted Pier Theatre. Clarkie sat in the stalls as we performed our entire repertoire. Clarkie called me down. 'I quite like you, my boy, but not the girl.'

Should my reply have been that he booked us both or not at all? I would have lost the job, so in truth I replied, 'Sir, I can always work single!'

At £12 a week, the contract was mine for 1940, as light comedian and straight man to Clarkie. But by 1940 the only theatre I was to be perform-ing in was a theatre of war.

The dreaded Uncle Lance decided that Sara was in grave danger from me, and to a lesser extent from the German bombs. He arranged an audi-tion for her with a Gilbert and Sullivan company that was leaving for Australia, and she secured the soubrette role. I got a job at the Colchester Rep. After two comedy roles, I was cast, still only 19, as Brabantio in *Othello*. The *Colchester Gazette* said, and I conceitedly quote, 'Richard Stone proved that his remarkable ability as a character actor can serve not only in comedy, but can reveal the dignity of a father's anger, for his Brabantio really lived'. Perhaps realistically, a notice in the *Colchester Gazette* is (like one in *The Stage*) about as much use as the Pope's b***s! Smaller parts, it said, were adequately filled by, amongst others, Paul Rogers. A few years ago that most distinguished of impresarios Michael Codron and I were discussing a co-star for my client, David Jason, in a new play. Michael suggested Paul Rogers and I asked him if he really wanted someone who 'adequately filled small parts' — rather than me, so impressive as Brabantio.

Sara left for Australia a few weeks later. I asked her to marry me as the train pulled out of Liverpool Street station, and she accepted. We were not to meet again for more than two years.

Soon after my twentieth birthday, early in 1940, I was called up and sent to a gunner training regiment at Deepcut near Aldershot. I wrote to Sara on my first day in the army.

928203 Gunner R Stone
D Battery R.A.
2nd Field Training Regiment
South Mindon Barracks
Deepcut
Hants

Sunday 18th

My own darling Child,

Here I am at Aldershot. How hectic it has all seemed — last night I was playing in *Othello* at this time, and here I am sitting in my blankets on the floor of an army hut at Aldershot . . . Then the biggest trial of the day, all my hair was SHORN OFF! Horror, I look like a convict. Then a piece of luck. I was called off Parade by a Captain Leather. He is in charge of Entertainments and had seen from my papers that I was an actor . . .

John Leather, with his wife Betty (an old pro), ran a theatre in Bromley. John drafted me into the concert party and then asked me to direct him and Betty in a production of *Close Quarters*, a two-handed play by Karel Stepanek. Every weekend, I was granted special leave, and driven by John to spend the time working on the play and staying in their beautiful home in Bromley.

The 12 weeks' training passed quickly enough, thanks to John Leather, whom I was not to meet again until 1946, when he reappeared in my life out of the blue and turned it upside down.

I was selected for OCTU (Officers Cadet Training Unit) and posted to Aldershot. An officer cadet is a chrysalis, neither an honest caterpillar nor a fully fledged butterfly. We had no rank, but sported a white band in our hats. The army specially selected a ruthless band of regular NCOs who were forced to call us 'sir', like 'Sir, you are a load of shit, sir, you'll never make a fucking officer, sir, you are a poofy bastard — SIR.'

To one particular sergeant who took us for drill, at what seemed to me, so recently an actor, to be the middle of the night, we would venture 'Good morning, Sergeant Muggeridge,' and his reply is Gunner history: 'Good morning. Fucking 'ell, sir, get fell in.' If you annoyed him any more, you were sent with a 25-pound shell under each arm to run around the perimeter of the parade ground. It was quite a surprise to pass out top of my intake, and a letter to Sara refers to this:

> The Colonel recommended to the War Office that I be posted to the Royal Horse Artillery Regiment. This is the highest compliment he could pay me my darling. It remains to be seen whether the War Office will take any notice. It seems rather odd that all this should happen to me who has neither done a stroke of work nor is even interested in it all beyond seeing it as something which must be done.

Most actors found themselves in some exotic and understanding regiment, like the Artists Rifles, but I was indeed posted to the Fifth Regiment Royal Horse Artillery. To give up their horses was the only concession the Horse Gunners had so far made to wartime soldiering. In every other respect they were maintaining the tradition and 'spit and polish' of a crack peacetime regiment.

I was to spend the next three years in CC Battery. The senior officers were all regular soldiers, so were the non-commissioned officers (sergeants and the like). It was hard enough for them to accept the influx of civilians. To get an actor was a worse disaster than Dunkirk!

My saviour was the Colonel. Rawdon Hoare was the one senior officer who was not strictly a regular soldier, having retired to civilian life between the wars. He was without doubt one of the most unusual regimental commanders in the British Army. In his forties, he was tall, thin, immaculate, and even in uniform looked and behaved like some pedantic monk who had been drafted into the army. His speech was precise and clipped. His movements were slightly mincing and he used his handkerchief as if playing in a Restoration comedy. He had no sexual interests either way and saw no reason why his officers should not suspend all such activities for the duration. His unique skill was to instil into us all a spirit of pride and devotion to the regiment, and to impose a most outrageously strict discipline.

The regiment was billeted at Great Easton near Dunmow, in a house built by Basil Dean, the theatrical producer, soon to become head of ENSA. Dean had converted a barn on his property into a theatre and Rawdon encouraged me to organise a concert. It amused him, but not other senior officers, to see me doing my act as a Girl Guide. I became Rawdon's 'court jester'. He liked to have me around and described me as 'a bee on a summer's afternoon'.

5RHA consisted of two regular batteries, K and G, and the new battery

CC added for the war. Accompanying Rawdon to an officers mess dinner at G Battery and being the junior subaltern present, I was seated at the very far end of the dining table. At the appropriate moment glasses were raised and the toast proposed, 'The King'. And the reply, which appeared to be unanimous, was 'God bless him!' I joined in. This was a serious social error. The major commanding G Battery glared the length of the table: 'The right to say "God bless him", Mr Stone, is reserved for officers of the rank of major and above.'

I felt like a character from a Bateman cartoon.

Surviving from my civilian wardrobe was a pair of gloves covered with long rabbit's fur. Officers were permitted to wear gloves on parade and there was nothing in king's regulations which stipulated what kind of gloves. My battery commander, one Ron Holman, didn't like me or my gloves. But Rawdon had smiled on them. Ron was a real creep and never one to cross the Colonel, so I wore them even into 'battle'. I'd bought an old banger in Aldershot for £15. When we moved to Yorkshire around Christmas 1940 the movement order specified 'lastly 2nd Lt Stone in his own car' and presumably in his own gloves! We were billeted in the bleak Yorkshire village of Silsden, in an unfurnished dingy terraced house. I was Messing Officer. In a letter to Sara I wrote:

> I went to an auction and bought some things for the mess. I got two armchairs for 17/6, two leather chairs for 4/-, a sofa for 6/6 and five walking sticks, a wash jug and basin, a coal scuttle, a chair and a table – all the lot for £2 ...

In Silsden I 'celebrated' my twenty-first birthday. The one bright spot in this dreary winter was the arrival of Gunner Farr. Before call-up Derek Farr had been a Rank Starlet. The Rank Organisation decided to premier his last film, *Quiet Wedding* in Leeds. Gunner Farr was collected in a chauffeur-driven Rolls and the officers followed in their uncomfortable open 15-hundredweight trucks.

After a spell in Chilton Foliat near Newbury, where I dallied with the vicar's daughter, we moved to Surrey, our final 'home' before going over- seas. The regiment was billeted in various villages on the road from Dorking to Guildford. CC Battery had the loveliest location of all, Wotton House, the original home of John Evelyn, the diarist. This beautiful seven- teenth-century mansion was set back from the main road on a long semi- circular drive and nestled on the edge of thick woods. Paths from the back of the house led to the pretty villages of Friday Street, Abinger Common and Holmbury St Mary. As Messing Officer for the men, I could draw a little cash in lieu of rations. I spent most of it in Dorking, but at a nearby watercress bed I bought vast amounts for practically nothing. We served 'watercress with everything'. I now learn I was known as Watercress Stone. We converted all leftovers from the week into brawn so that the 'buffet' on Saturdays was corned beef, spam, brawn and of course watercress!

Rawdon Hoare was in his element. Our guns were polished until they shone. The rubber tyres were black-leaded. Each gun emplacement was encircled by shining white rope. Once a week Rawdon inspected this charade, and by remembering the name and personal problems of the oldest sergeant and the newest recruit, mesmerised us and we worshipped him. At the end of a normal day's work, Rawdon saw no reason why his officers should seek the company of women, even their wives. So to prevent this, he summoned us to shooting practice on miniature ranges, depicting the hills, forests and villages where some day it was assumed we would be firing our guns. It was a terrible experience to direct the fire of imaginary guns with an audience consisting of Rawdon and the regular officers. Puffs of smoke would rise where the shells had supposedly landed. My practice shots occasionally obliterated our own infantry.

Derek Farr was at that time married to Carole Lynne, now Lady Delfont. Carole was opening in a Leslie Julian Jones revue, *Rise Above It*, starring the two Hermiones – Baddeley and Gingold – at the Criterion Theatre, which, being totally underground, was one of a few London theatres now allowed to open. Derek had seats for the opening night, and asked me rather tentatively if we could go together, having already obtained 'compassionate leave' for the evening. Thinking it was highly unlikely that Ron Holman would countenance Second Lieutenant Stone hobnobbing with Gunner Farr, I obtained an evening's leave on some totally different excuse. Derek walked from Wotton House, ostensibly to catch the bus to Dorking, whilst I drove my car and picked him up once safely out on the Dorking road!

I was terribly lonely and felt that I might be posted overseas and never see Sara again, and then a letter of hers got me in a panic. I wrote back:

> My whole world has turned upside down this morning because in your letter. I saw the gleam of a possibility that you might be falling in love with Michael – do please, darling remember how much we loved each other. How complete our happiness was. There can never be a greater happiness than that. I shall love you for always.

Sara's diary at the time contains her side of the story. 'Miserable about not going back to England – why did I give up my chance of happiness. I'll go next year somehow'. And then, what do you know, the next day, September 23rd, 'Michael phoned asked me to marry him.'

I think two dozen orchids and a telegram saved the day. It read:

SARA GREGORY GILBERT AND SULLIVAN MELBOURNE
ARE YOU FALLING IN LOVE WITH MICHAEL STOP OUR
LOVE IS TOO GREAT TO SPOIL STOP I SHALL WAIT
ALWAYS STOP WIRE RICHARD.

To secure a passage Sara needed an offer of work in England. She got one from Herbert Farjeon to appear in his new revue *Light and Shade*. In January 1942, on the night of the dress rehearsal of *Lilac Time*, in which she was to star in Sydney, Sara was offered a cabin on a tramp steamer, bound for England. Sir Frank Tait, the benign head of J.C. Williamson, the leading Australian management, generously released her. After passing through the Panama Canal the ship hid from German submarines each night at different ports up the east coast of America, before joining a convoy to cross the Atlantic.

I was on embarkation leave in the Cotswolds when Sara's boat finally docked at Liverpool. I was at the pictures. When I returned, my father was polishing my Sam Browne belt and gave me the news. Taking the first train for London in the morning, I was met by my troop commander, who drove me to Redhill, where Sara was staying with yet another aunt. When we met, we both had a strong urge to run away from the daunting prospect of tying ourselves for life to someone whom we had not seen for over two years. Nevertheless, on 28th April 1942, we were married in St John's Church, Redhill. We had one week together and then parted again for another two years. I wrote a few days later on board ship:

What a wonderful week we had. When first of all we searched for each other not quite remembering, not quite understanding, readjusting our almost childlike memories. Then we were gloriously happy like any other honeymoon couple, and then we remembered that we were going to be parted again and gained strength and happiness from God. My darling, that week just about saved my rather tottering faith in a lot of things. I am going to this job with your love and everything that that love inspired.

5

*My active service in the Western Desert and Italy,
including the worst day of my life and being wounded*

5RHA was now part of the Eighth Armoured Division and, having been
issued with tropical kit, we assumed that we were not going to Iceland!
The regiment embarked on a small American pleasure boat, the SS
Borinquen, which in view of the drastic shortage of shipping at this crucial
time in the war had been brought out of retirement and was serving as a
troop carrier. No-one, but no-one, supports my memory of it being a flat-
bottomed Mississippi paddle steamer. It certainly behaved like one in the
Bay of Biscay. We were, of course, on our way to the Middle East, but it
was too dangerous at this time to go through the Mediterranean so we
went right round Africa. In Capetown, where we thrilled to well-stocked
shops and blazing lights, we changed ships. We left on the *Monarch of
Bermuda*, a pre-war luxury liner with restaurants, stewards and fabulous
food. Whoopee, sharing the boat was a field hospital with a bunch of
comely nurses. There were dances in the ballroom. Then disaster: Rawdon
issued an order that officers of 5RHA were forbidden to fraternise with
female members of the Royal Army Medical Corps! We objected, and a
deputation of me and one other junior officer approached Rawdon. After a
lengthy argument the order was withdrawn with the proviso that, like
Cinderella, we were to be in our own cabins before the stroke of midnight.

In a BBC broadcast Churchill cheered the nation, with the news that the
'Might of England' was now on its way to the Middle East, to chase
Rommel out of Egypt across the African desert and into the Mediterranean
Sea. Sadly, the Might of England was only us, the Eighth Armoured
Division equipped with antiquated tanks and guns from the 1914/18 war.
Furthermore, the Commanding General and his entire staff had been put,
in error, on a ship bound for India. There was a considerable delay when
we arrived in Egypt whilst they reshipped our bosses back from Bombay
to Alexandria!

War should be fought in the desert, where towns are not destroyed and little children killed. In North Africa we chased Rommel to Benghazi and he chased us back, and we both fired away and mostly made holes in the desert. Casualties were not high, and a great mutual respect existed between the two armies.

In the summer of '42, Rommel was at the gates of Cairo. Monty had not yet arrived, and the division was involved in some unsuccessful actions. I was now a 'gun position officer' in charge of four guns. I lived in my 15-hundredweight truck with Driver McDowell, Bombardier Bartley (my technical assistant) and wireless operator Lapidus, who received our orders to fire from our troop commander a mile or so ahead with the tanks. I think its really something that Frank Bartley, Leslie Lapidus and I still meet after over 50 years, at our annual reunions. There is a heart-warming postscript to all this. McDowell died and his son wrote a letter to a North Country paper asking if any of his comrades from the Western Desert remembered his father. Leslie Lapidus happened to see the letter and got in touch with McDowell junior, who joined us at a reunion.

In the desert we acquired a fifth companion, a chicken we called Monty. She lived on the wireless set. She was mentioned in several of my letters:

Monty refused to get in when we moved yesterday – very nearly got left behind. The Sergeant Major rounded her up and brought her along in his truck.

Monty perched on my hat whilst I was giving out orders the other day, and then did her stuff all over me.

Monty has started laying eggs. She laid the first one the day after Tunis fell.

Monty gets tamer. Sits on our shoulders and flies into the back when we move off.

Monty failed to get on board when we moved today, she was run over by Sgt Short's gun and we ate her!

At a very recent reunion Leslie Lapidus said that he must make a confession to me before he died. It appears that he had purchased Monty from an Arab with one of my spare shirts! McDowell was our cook and did the best he could to disguise our rations. A gooey mass of bully beef and hard biscuits boiled in a drop of water was known as 'biscuit burgoo'. We were, in theory, allowed two pints of water each per day for drinking, washing and shaving, but on so many occasions the containers were leaky or the water had nearly evaporated. Despite the intense heat of the African desert in the day, it became very cold at night, with a heavy dew. We crawled, fully clothed except for our boots, into our sleeping bags, but it was preferable to be under cover. There was room in the back of the truck for Leslie and Frank. McDowell and I attached a roll of canvas to either side of the truck, which we unfurled and pegged to the ground to provide us each with a makeshift tent.

The African desert is not only sand, but stony, with a sparse covering of hopeless tiny bushes, and then suddenly a few threadbare palm trees and an oasis of water.

Miles from anywhere, an Arab would seemingly pop out of the ground with a handful of eggs, offering 'Eggis for tea'. The exchange of a couple of eggs for used tea leaves satisfied both parties.

Monty (the real Monty, not our chicken) had been sent out to take command of the Eighth Army. Enough has been written of his effect on the course of the war; let me only add that his effect on us was mesmeric. Oddly dressed, even by desert rat standards, with a capful of badges, he looked and sounded like a parrot in fancy dress. Within minutes he had wiped the silly smile from our faces. The words 'if' and 'when' were missing from his vocabulary. He told us that on a certain date, in a certain place he *would* attack and he *would* succeed – and we believed him, and rightly so. Waiting for Alamein, we grasped such fun as was available. We bathed in the Mediterranean and the officer's mess was re-established in the open air on plain wooden tables. We would eat our bully beef and biscuits served in style by the same bombardier mess waiter from Wotton. Beer for the men, whisky for the officers, was the ration, all accompanied by a great army of flies who would gather on the glasses and cups and when you drank would fall in! It's not surprising that so many of us went down with jaundice, including me. I was bright yellow and spent a couple of weeks in a hospital in the suburbs of Cairo. I had a room on the corner of the first floor and looked down on two open-air cinemas. Egyptian films ain't Spielberg! A week's sick leave in Shepheard's Hotel brought home the incredible contrast in the lives of the fighting soldiers in the desert and those with 'cushy jobs' enjoying the fleshpots of Cairo.

5RHA were now part of the Seventh Armoured Division. Proudly we were desert rats. The Battle of Alamein turned the tide of the Second World War, and we started the long advance west. The difficulty of a swift advance in the desert, covering hundreds of miles, is one of supply. Gradually the amount of troops that could be provisioned with food, water and ammunition got less and less. When we reached the mountain range of El Agheila, only 400 miles from Tripoli, the army had been reduced to a brigade of tanks supported by 5RHA. El Agheila was Rommel's last major stand before Tripoli. He had festooned the hills with his deadly 88-millimetre guns and our tanks were in trouble. We advanced across a vast plain and Harry Troop was deployed in full view of the enemy. Our object was to knock out the guns on the hill, so that the tanks could advance. We

33

443

BUCKINGHAM PALACE.

Admit one to witness the

Investiture

(at 10.15 o'clock a.m.)

- 9 MAY 1944

Lord Chamberlain.

were under deadly accurate fire from the moment we took up our position. It was probably the worst day of my life. I was to see two of my four guns receive direct hits and a great number of my men killed or wounded. But we stayed put and kept firing and eventually Rommel withdrew and our tanks moved forward over the ridge of El Agheila. I received a Military Cross for that awful day, but it belongs to the men who died.

I have a mental picture of Rawdon Hoare, a middle-aged visitor to that dreadful carnage, standing in his immaculately pressed tropical shorts with his faithful batman at his side, sipping a cup of tea. He may not have known quite what was going on but it was he who had instilled into us the discipline not to pack it in, and his presence in the most dangerous spot he could have found, looking like some visiting bishop, was inspiring.

At El Agheila, Willy, my troop commander, was wounded, and I was 'promoted' and sent up to take over directing the fire of the guns. I was not very good at it, and in one minor skirmish I brought the shells perilously close to the tanks I was meant to be supporting! I nearly killed a young New Zealand captain who poked his head out of his tank at the wrong moment. However, Nigel Neilson and I became good friends. I looked after him as an actor after the war. He had a persuasive personality and always got the job. The performance was not so good. He was such a good friend and going nowhere that, for the first and last time in my career, I persuaded an actor to pack it in. He went into PR, becoming right-hand man to Onassis and made a fortune.

We acquired a new battery commander. He became General Sir Brian Wyldbore-Smith, but I cannot square this with the rumbustious friendly humorous man who sang childishly rude songs in his cups! A welcome change from Ron. I met him recently at a Desert Rats Reunion; he hadn't changed. I bet him 50 quid he wouldn't come to a regimental reunion and sing his rude song. He hasn't turned up so far, but we did sing it together in

1999 on our way to Woolwich to celebrate the regiment's 60th birthday!

By Christmas 1942 we were 100 miles from Tripoli, but unable to advance further as the supply lines up from Cairo were stretched to their limit. We were existing on the barest rations and ammunition was non-existent. If Rommel had attacked then we could once more have been running back the other way. A couple more quotes from air letters:

> We ran out of baking powder in the cookhouse today so we made a pudding with Andrews Liver Salts. I haven't seen any of the men who ate it yet.

> I wonder what Christmas will hold for us out here. I've ordered the most colossal amount of turkey pies, pudding etc. but wonder if they will fetch it up all this way.

> BUT

> On Monty's personal orders, the Air Force flew up a full Christmas dinner, with turkey, plum pudding, mince pies, booze the lot!
>
> Nigel Neilson and I, hopefully, rounded off a remarkable day by organising and performing a fairly impromptu concert on the back of a lorry.

On the last advance before we captured Tripoli I was wounded, while still 'holding the fort' for Willy. Sitting on top of my tank, we were suddenly attacked by a lone German Stuka, a tiny fighter plane much feared by desert rats as it flew so low, machine-gunning and dropping bombs from a few feet above the ground. I received shrapnel wounds but our tank's machine-guns brought down the Stuka when it came in for a second run. I then had the unusual experience of being sent down the line to hospital with the pilot. Three letters to Sara and a telegram record the day, the first an airgraph. These were written on a foolscap-sized form, photo-graphed and sent to England as a microscopic piece of film, then enlarged and delivered. For interest, here is exactly what Sara received plus a transcript to explain my scrawl.

> My very own darling Sara. I'm afraid I am on my way back to hospi-tal darling. I unfortunately got too close to a bomb and got some wee splinters in me!
>
> There's absolutely nothing to worry about. I have no pain at all and all it amounts to is about four tiny flesh wounds.
>
> I had the extraordinary experience of sleeping the night in the A.O.S. near to the Stuka pilot who bombed us and was later brought down.

35

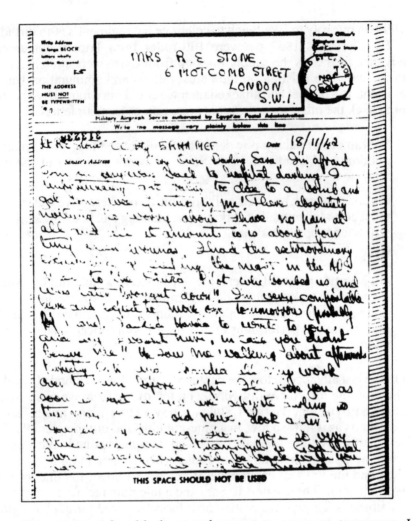

I'm very comfortable here and expect to move on tomorrow. I asked Harold to write to you to say that I wasn't hurt, in case you didn't believe me!!

He saw me walking about afterwards, perfectly OK and I handed all my work over to him before I left. I'll wire you as soon as I get anywhere definite darling so this may be all old news.

Look after yourself, darling I love you so very much and I'm so thankful to God I was so lucky and will be back with you again.

With all my love *Richard*

And another airmail letter:

36

I'm getting back to base in hops. I've so far done two plane trips and am now waiting in a casualty clearing station for the last lap, and still by my side the Stuka pilot. I came terribly near to cracking after I'd been wounded, and he came over again as my wounds were being dressed!! The last lap was by train, still with the Stuka pilot. We smiled and chatted a little in my broken German and were parted when the train reached Cairo, he to go to a prisoner-of-war hospital, I to be sent, this time, to a tented hospital south of Cairo.

And a letter:

In hospital at last! Sheets, flowers and china plates!

And here is the final evidence from the saga of my injuries.

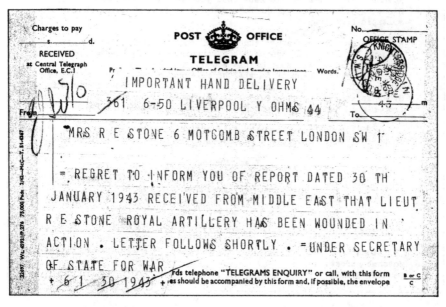

I recuperated at Lady Lampson's Home for Officers on the Nile. Enjoying the comforts of Cairo after being wounded felt better than missing El Alamein with yellow jaundice! Yet eating cream cakes in Groppi's, I still felt some scorn, tinged perhaps with jealousy for those who eat there every day. When I got back to the regiment Tripoli had fallen, and we were on our way through Tunisia to meet head on the American First Army, who had landed in north-west Africa. The almost unopposed drive west was enlivened by thousands of Italians, who couldn't wait to surrender, hands in the air waving and laughing.

Any further communication on this subject
should be addressed to :—

   The Under Secretary of State,
     The War Office,
       The Casualty Branch,
         Blue Coat School,
           Church Road,
             Wavertree,
              Liverpool 15.

and the following number quoted :

   OS/4362/S
  ....(Casualties)

THE WAR OFFICE,

CASUALTY BRANCH,

BLUE COAT SCHOOL,

CHURCH ROAD,

WAVERTREE,

LIVERPOOL, 15.

6th February, 1943.

Madam,

      In confirmation of War Office telegram dated the 3rd February, 1943, I regret to have to inform you that a report dated the 30th January, 1943, has been received by telegraph from the Military Authorities in the Middle East that your husband, Lieutenant R.E. Stone, Royal Artillery, has been wounded in action having sustained multiple bomb wounds.

      No particulars as to the name of the hospital to which your husband has been admitted have been furnished. If, however, he becomes seriously ill as a result of his wounds, further reports will be received by telegraph which will be telegraphed on to you. In the absence of such a communication, it can be assumed that Lieutenant Stone is making normal progress in which event you will, no doubt, hear from him in due course about his progress.

      Will you kindly acquaint this office of any change in your address, in case further reports are received.

                I am, Madam,
                Your obedient Servant,

                A. Williams

Mrs. R.E. Stone,
  6, Motcomb Street,
    London, S.W.1.

A letter dated 11/5/43:

This battle is over now. Someone else is rounding up the remaining Germans. I gave the order which landed the first shell in Tunis. When we drove in the whole population were lining the streets cheering and waving and the girls flinging their arms around our necks. I found a hotel to get a drink, a barber to get a hair cut and a milliner to buy you a hat which was brought from Paris only last November.

The Seventh Armoured Division was pulled back 100 miles east of Tripoli near a village called Homs. There was a great need during this 'resting' period for entertainment. Lieutenant Cecil Clarke and I were 'borrowed' from our regiments and became the Entertainments Officers. Before the war and afterwards 'Clarkie' had a distinguished career in show business, both with the legendary Michel St Denis and later as head of special drama projects with Lew Grade's ATV.

We were extremely lucky to have at Homs a Roman amphitheatre – Leptis Magna. It was in a marvellous state of preservation. The stage area, with its tall pillars, some still intact, was still usable. At the back, behind the pillars, we were able to arrange dressing rooms. The auditorium was a steeply sloping tiered semi-circle. Performers could stand on the stage below, as they had done 2,000 years before, and the same Mediterranean breeze blowing off the sea wafted every word without amplification to the back of the vast auditorium. As it seated 8,000, it was only necessary to give one performance of each show, so that our task was not easy.

There were a few divisional concert parties around, including The Balmorals from the Highland Division, featuring the distinguished critic and journalist, Felix Barker, and The Black Cats from the 56th Division. This latter was presided over by Second Lieutenant Richard Gilbert, who was Africa's version of Gloria in *It Ain't Arf Ot, Mum*. When not in drag, he was an exceptionally brave infantry officer, leading his men with the campest of battle-cries. We formed a dance band, the Rat-Tat-Tats and I introduced innumerable variety shows with talent from the division. One of my topical gags concerned the British Tommy who picked up a girl in Tripoli, but was told 'the V is for Victory, but the bundles are not for Britain'.

There were also the occasional ENSA shows, some only four-handed, the remnants of pre-war concert parties from the smaller resorts (like Saltburn!) who had been in the desert for years in conditions no better than the fighting soldiers'. We billeted the artistes in a small house by the sea on the edge of the village. After a show by one of those parties, I decided to spend the night on a camp bed on the verandah, presumably to guard the honour of the English ladies of ENSA. It was a useless gesture. A mature lady accordionist crept into my bed in the middle of the night and, without too much resistance, I was raped.

Nothing so undignified occurred when ENSA's all-star party arrived with Olivier, Vivien Leigh, Leslie Henson and Beatrice Lillie. This was a great occasion. I shall never forget bathing with Bea Lillie. She tied a handkerchief over her upper half, and wore one of the little round fez-like hats for which she was so famous. They gave two shows in the amphitheatre to 8,000 people and we gave them dinner in the ruins. Clarkie did the lighting. The pillars at the back of the theatre were lit from the stage – it was quite wonderful.

Monty, in spite of criticism from the press, the church and the soldiers' wives, authorised the establishment of brothels. The brothel in Homs was to be under the joint control of the Medical Corps and Army Entertainments. I was despatched, with a captain from the RAMC, to choose 25 eligible prostitutes from Tripoli. I was to choose them for their pulchritude, the doctor for their health. We made our selection and bundled the ladies into the back of a 3-ton lorry. One hundred miles on a bumpy desert road is a long way. They asked us to stop for a pee. It was at this moment that a convoy of the Highland Division passed by, to the delight of several hundred randy Scotsmen!

Homs was a tiny seaside village and Clarkie and I requisitioned the best house on the front as our headquarters, where we lived in enviable comfort. Up the road were the cinema and brothel, both under our control. The cinema only held 400. We played the films non-stop except for a short break when the projector became overheated. Roughly the same procedure applied in the brothel. But this idyllic summer of 1943, playing at show business, was to end. I was recalled to 5RHA, and a short burst of intensive training for the next campaign.

We landed at Salerno and were to fight our way up Italy from October to early December. It was bliss to pick peaches and tomatoes and to eat fresh vegetables again, but there was another side to it, and I wrote:

I am sitting in a beautiful green field and the view is of miles of orchards and vineyards and the most wonderful mountains. There is a little village clinging to the side of the nearest mountain but I know that village which looks like a glittering white sprawling fairy castle is nothing but a shell. It's hell to be fighting in this lovely land – I hate sending our shells to destroy villages. In the desert there was no beauty to be destroyed.

Our bank manager had written to Sara saying he was glad she was going to start work again. He had today received her family lodging allowance from 1st October 1942 to 31st August 1943 amounting to £15 0s 4d! Despite this, the account only showed a credit balance of £54 5s 5d.

Sara opened on tour in September and in view of our precarious finances booked herself into cheap digs. My mother disapproved, and so did I, especially when I heard on the grapevine that her elderly leading man (young leading men were in the forces) was hell-bent on extending their stage romance into the bedroom!

I wrote:

Darling there is one thing that worried me in a letter from Mother. She said that you were staying in cheap digs. Please don't. I think I had better explain what I earn and how much you can spend. I am now paid 14/6 per day and 4/- Marriage Allowance and 2/- Field Allowance and 1/9 Colonial Allowance which comes to £7.14 a week. I spend about £3.00 which leaves £4.00 for you.

We were finally to go back to Sorrento, where as Messing Officer I arranged a battery dinner in a five-star hotel. It was a fabulous affair, served off white tablecloths with the hotel's best silver. It was 18 months since we had landed in Egypt and the battery had sat down to a decent meal.

We embarked for home in December and docked in Gourock in January 1944. I wrote to Sara: 'I'm in England, not wounded or sick, just come home!'

I didn't know it then, but my time as a fighting soldier was over. The rest of my life was to be in the land of make-believe. My best memories are of my troop of gunners. Ordinary men, accepting their duty and steeling themselves to war. Ordinary men, behaving without greed, or lies, or ambition, in perfect comradeship.

Extraordinary men.

MISS SARA GREGORY
6 MOTCOMB STREET
— LONDON
ENGLAND   S.W.I.

Military Airgraph Service authorised by Egyptian Postal Administration
Write the message very plainly below this line

PASSED

Lt. Richard Stone., M.O. No.1.General Hospital, MEF. 20th March 1945.

Sender's Address   To-day I received yet another bill for my Khaki Drill.
I am therefore forced to write an ....

ANSWER TO A TAILOR'S BILL.

Dear Mr. Austin Mowe,
I hope this won't find you as it leaves me now.
I hasten to tell you my awful mishap. Well,
My battle-dress jacket is riddled with shrapnel.

But though I feel cold on a wintry night,
(As a bald man wearing a collander might)
I'm happy to think that your lovely creations
Will still be immune from the wrath of the nations.

Your lovely creations will stay stored away
In your ant-proof tin box at Base Depot, R.A.
And before, Mr. Mowe, I go back to the wars
I shall change this old jacket at Hospital Stores.

"Khaki Drill jacket and two pairs of trousers.
Everyone's taking at least two pairs, now sir."
But Jerry treats them the same somehow,
Be they W.D., or Austin Mowe.

Trying the topes on was fun,
Though I've never seen anyone wearing one.
And topes long and topes short
Were among the "useful" things I bought.

When the war has ceased between the nations,
I shall send you back your lovely creations.
And, Mr. Mowe, you needn't claim,
If the ant-proof box has failed its name.

P.S. If Jim is really coming out here, you'd
better send him a copy of this.

42

6

'Stars in Battledress', meeting the daunting Mrs George Formby and Benny Hill, giving Frankie Howerd the thumbs-down, and teaming up with Ian Carmichael

Sara had been working steadily whilst I was away. After the Farjeon revue she got a larger role in the revival of *The Vagabond King* starring Webster Booth and Anne Ziegler. With their signature tune 'Only a Rose' Anne and Leslie (Webster) were a big draw then, topping variety bills all over the country. Their recordings of love duets topped the 'charts'.

The Vagabond King was at the Winter Gardens (now the New London and home of *Cats*). It was the first job as a director for Robert Nesbitt, who was later to become famous for his spectacular revues in London. He loved lighting his shows. At one dress rehearsal there was a pot of paint in the middle of the stage. 'Strike that,' shouted the stage manager. 'No,' someone yelled back. 'For God's sake no. Mr Nesbitt has lit it!'

Sara played opposite Sid Walker, a famous radio comedian of the day with his catchphrase 'any rags, bottles or bones'. His son, Peter Walker, after the war made dozens of low-budget horror films, into which he inveigled my distinguished actors to appear at much reduced fees by phoning me at my office at 7 p.m. with tomorrow's casting – a nurse for £25, a tart for £20 and a judge for £30.

Her next engagement was with the fabulous Robert Atkins. She played Titania to his Bottom and was nightly sexually harassed on the grassy bank. Robert Atkins and Donald Wolfit were legends. They were the last of the actor-managers with their own touring companies playing the classics. If anything, Robert's supporting cast was tattier even than Donald's. A friend came round to Robert's dressing room in the interval and remarked that the king seemed a little tipsy. 'Laddie, if you think the king was drunk wait till you see the Duke of Buckingham.'

When we landed in Gourock Sara was playing *Cinderella* in Southsea. I telephoned during a performance. Her Prince Charming, answered the phone, which was in the wings, and asked me to hang on as Sara was on stage. For the first time in two years I could hear her voice. She was singing 'Long Ago and Faraway'.

After my embarkation leave in Southsea I decided I'd done enough fighting and could justifiably apply for a transfer to something in Entertainment. Whereupon I was to meet someone else who was to play an important part in my life. Major Basil Brown was critical of the value of ENSA to the actual fighting soldiers, maintaining that the best seldom reached the front line. ENSA tended to place its stars in full-scale productions, which then only played garrison theatres in large towns. There were exceptions like George Formby, Tommy Trinder, Alice Delysia and Joyce Grenfell, who insisted on doing their shows as far forward as possible. Joyce Grenfell brought not only her pianist and her songs and monologues, but her sunny personality and smile to the smallest hospital ward of wounded soldiers. Mainly it was the smallest shows built from the remnants of the seaside concert parties which reached the front line. ENSA was said to stand for 'Every Night Something Awful'.

Basil realised that there were in the army a number of professional artistes, most of them unfit for active service, who were wasting their talents working as clerks or cleaning out latrines. For two years he had fought a campaign at the War Office to mobilise this talent into 'Stars in Battledress'. At the time of my interview, there were a dozen parties in rehearsal under captains George and Alfred Black, at The Central Pool of Artistes in Chelsea Barracks. Basil was promoted Lieutenant Colonel and appointed ADAWS (Assistant Director Army Welfare Services) ENTS 21 Army Group. The job which he gave me carried no such title, nor did it carry much rank. I was to be Staff Captain Welfare (Ents) Second Army.

Sara was on tour again with *The Waltz Dream*. Her young lover in this was Derek Oldham, star of the first London production of *Rose Marie* a long time ago. Whilst Sara was away, I shared with her flatmate, the delicious Carol Raye, their Whitelands House flat, and commuted daily to army headquarters in Victoria. Sara did not fancy this arrangement and we rented our first 'home', a studio at 104 Ebury Street, behind a lodging house. It had a corrugated-iron roof over the studio area in which we lived and slept. Behind and down three stairs was a small airless kitchen and bathroom. Gunner Chitty, my batman in 5RHA whom I had managed to bring with me to Second Army, looked after me whilst Sara was on tour. He was a professional gardener and still had his connections in the country. He cooked enormous bowls of rhubarb, on which I existed until they developed a white crust and had to be ditched.

In army welfare there were too many chiefs and not enough Indians. At 21 Army Group there was a brigadier in charge, with a gaggle of colonels, one each for Live Entertainment (Basil), Radio (Eric 'A Nightingale Sang in Berkeley Square' and 'These Foolish Things' Maschwitz), Kinema

Admin, etc. etc. Under them a host of majors, captains and lieutenants wandering about looking lost. At Second Army, one step down the line, where all the work was done, there was one lieutenant colonel and two staff captains, Jimmy Kennedy and I. Jimmy, a lovely Irishman who had composed a string of popular ballads, including 'South of the Border' and 'Red Sails in the Sunset', was Colonel Loman's right-hand man, whilst I dealt with Entertainment.

Basil had decided that 'Stars in Battledress' units were to be on the beachheads with the first wave of troops, and I was to lead them into battle! It was therefore on D-Day plus four that Captain Stone, still only 24, found himself on a tank-landing craft with the most absurd army ever to go into battle. The Normandy beachheads were far from secure. The 'Stars in Battledress' units consisted of Terry Thomas, Arthur Haynes, Charlie Chester and sundry other comedians, jugglers, conjurors and musicians, who were mostly unfit for active service and should not have been within a hundred miles of any invasion. There were even three teenage ATS girls. Frances Tanner, of the Tanner Sisters was one, and another, the clever impressionist Janet Brown. We waded ashore carrying our make-up, props and musical instruments, and dragging mini pianos. We stood forlornly on the beachhead whilst enemy shells were falling around us. I was the idiotic leader of a band of musicians who had got the date wrong and turned up a week early for the dance.

It was gloriously summed up by Cyril Lagey, the black drummer with 'Sergeant Sid Millward and his Nitwits', an incredibly funny band, which is still touring America, although they must all be in their eighties. A 'red-tabbed' brigadier, puzzled by this pile of bizarre theatrical equipment and lounging thespians, approached Lagey and asked, 'What on earth are you doing here?'

Lagey's reply was a classic: 'Sir, that's what I've been asking myself all day.'

Terry Thomas, on the beachhead with a cigarette in a long holder, was right to tell us, 'You're an absolute shower!'

Wilfred Hyde White was there too in a play, wearing the very thick overcoat that for years he wore on tour, even in the tropics.

Arthur Haynes was later to become part of the 'Charlie Chester Radio Gang' and then a television star with his own show. He was, in my opinion, an underrated comic; his sketches with Nicholas Parsons, whom he addressed always as Nicholarse, were comic gems. He was part wide-boy, part innocent. He even survived the inclusion of the girlfriend of Val Parnell, his TV boss, who sang a solo right off key in every show in the series, which ran for several years until Arthur died.

Eventually, as the beachheads became secure, I managed to get some transport for my motley crew. Having requisitioned an unoccupied monastery outside Bayeux, we set up our headquarters. Within a few days the war had stabilised enough for us to start performing, and for Basil's dream to be fulfilled. The first 'Stars in Battledress' party performed within a week of our landing and within one mile of the Germans!

Our Colonel, Russell Loman, was a dynamic little man with a face like a benevolent frog. He had, before the war, been working for the Gas Board and his face had been the model for 'Mr Therm'. It was quite clear to Russell that welfare, like charity, began at home. He was the most loveable rogue ever to escape long-term imprisonment in the Second World War.

NAAFI had sent over gift packs, which were destined, until Russell got hold of them, to be distributed free to the troops. Russell decided that this was too generous so he gave instructions for them to be opened and the contents to be sold to the troops as individual items. He set up 'gift shops' as we advanced from Normandy to Brussels. Starting modestly with local produce, such as Camembert cheese and perfume, he became more ambitious. Convoys of 3-ton lorries were sent down to the Charente to return loaded with cognac.

'Stars in Battledress' were now doing a good job and ENSA parties began to arrive. Much to the annoyance of Basil Dean, they were placed for the first time under an army officer – me! The emotive subject was 'routeing'. Throughout the war Dean and his civilian ENSA officers had virtually chosen where they would perform. Now the army had control and he didn't like it. I rushed forward with an ENSA party headed by Flanagan and Allen, Florence Desmond and the pianist, Kay Cavendish, so that we arrived in Brussels on the Wednesday it was liberated. At the ABC theatre the posters were still on display for the German opera company which had not concluded its week's engagement. It read 'Monday, Tuesday, Wednesday, *Rosenkavalier*. Thursday, Friday and Saturday '*Cavalleria, Rusticana* and *Pagliacci*'.

I slipped the bills with, 'Flanagan and Allen' and we opened on Thursday.

I wrote a couple of days later:

I have had a wild week, darling, moving almost every other day – dragging the Flanagan and Allen party along with me. I saw Paris one day – it is unbelievably gay, with hundreds of people on brightly coloured bicycles and all the women are too lovely and beautifully dressed after four years of German occupation. We then rushed ahead to Brussels and handed round day bills and broadcast on the diffusion van and result was an enormous house in the biggest theatre we had opened so far. With Jimmy Kennedy in front, Flanagan and Allen sang 'Home Town' and introduced Jimmy as the

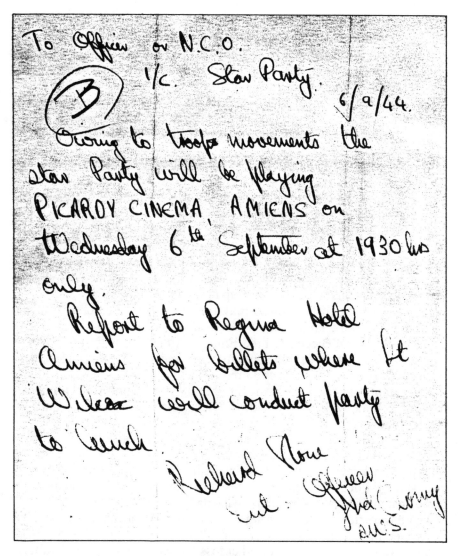

To Officer or N.C.O.

(B) I/c. Star Party. 6/9/44.

Owing to troops movements the Star Party will be playing PICARDY CINEMA, AMIENS on Wednesday 6th September at 1930 hrs only.

Report to Regina Hotel Amiens for billets where Lt Wilcox will conduct party to lunch.

Richard Stone
Lieut. Officer i/c.
E.N.S.

composer, Bud and Ches are going home tomorrow, I'm sorry it has been a thrill having them with us. Nothing was too much trouble. When I think of George Formby!

I can only think from my remark about George Formby that Beryl must have been there! I got to know them well after the war. George wouldn't hurt a fly, Beryl was a monster. I can imagine her giving me a very rough time indeed.

The liberation of Brussels was a night to remember, the whole population went wild. We danced in the streets and later were invited by generous Belgians to share their houses and their daughters. We set up our Welfare Headquarters in Brussels. So began the first serious hiccup of our married life. I needed civilian staff and in came Feré. She was more than a secretary but it seemed to go unnoticed that we arrived together at the office each day in my car. She was a redhead with a lovely figure and I brushed up my French in the best classroom in the world. Soon 21 Army Group Headquarters came to take over in Brussels and we advanced, and Feré came too.

Somehow my letters to Sara must have contained too little mention of the hardships of war. Her tour with Derek was over, and she was con-tracted for pantomime at the London Coliseum, but there were still six weeks 'vacant'. Without warning, she applied to ENSA for a short engagement and was allotted the Middle East. This was not the object of the exercise, strings were pulled, and she was posted to ENSA Pool of Artistes in Brussels! In the little Dutch town of Wiert, accompanied by Feré, I visited the newly arrived ENSA party to find it included my wife! It was not an easy meeting and I gave up my secretary.

Sara went back to London to play the title role in pantomime at the London Coliseum quaintly called *Goody Two Shoes*. The top star of this epic was that great eccentric, Fred Emney. I think it was the *New Yorker* that said 'There are three things not to be missed in London, Buckingham Palace, the Tower of London and Fred Emney.'

Regrettably one is now missing. Fred Emney the enormous barrage bal-loon of a man with the chuckling deep voice, the monocle and the Churchillian cigar.

Fred, had the 'number one' dressing room at the Coliseum on the stage level, Sara had number six, up several flights of stairs. By the middle of March, Sara knew she was pregnant with our first son, Barry. She was very sick and dear Fred gave her his dressing room and dragged his 20 stone up and down all those stairs twice daily.

There were fierce battles during the last stages of the war in Europe, but my concern was the deployment of 'Stars in Battledress' and ENSA parties as Second Army advanced across the Rhine and up to Hamburg. Russell Loman was becoming bolder. His mistress was established in a boutique in Brussels, for which he supplied delightful leather handbags that were also featured in his army gift shops. Some of the lorries with the brandy from Cognac found their way to a friendly nightclub where he lavishly entertained other senior officers. When we captured the little town of Celle, I requisitioned a large dump of white parachute silk. It would have been invaluable for costumes and theatre curtains, but Russell saw to it that only a small amount was given to me. Jimmy Kennedy and I asked what was to happen to the remainder, and were assured, that it would be made into shirts and nightdresses for the gift shops. This we believed, until one night the telephone rang in the tent I shared with Jimmy. The call came from the Belgian/Dutch frontier. Could we explain the meaning of three 10-ton lorries containing rolls of pure white silk addressed to a shop in Brussels? We hastily assured the astonished military police officer on the other end of the line that there must have been a misunderstanding. These lorries were of course meant to go to Lieutenant Colonel Basil Brown, at 21 Army Group and would he please re-route them there. Basil was surprised and delighted and re-curtained every garrison theatre in Europe!

However, Russell's activities began to attract suspicion and he was up for a court martial. But he had entertained so lavishly and given brandy and leather handbags and nightdresses to so many senior officers (for their wives, I hope) that he had to be spirited away and the affair hushed up. He was promoted and posted, as a full colonel, to be the Town Major of Copenhagen. The mind boggles at the opportunities opened up to him. I have never seen him since!

On VE Day, Second Army Headquarters was on the Luneburg Heath. I wrote:

> Tuesday VE Night – the war is over. Outside the troops have lit a huge bonfire and they are letting off rockets. The DCLI Band is playing and I have arranged for Dorothy Carless to come and sing to them.

Dorothy Carless's accompanist was a 20-year-old Cyril Ornadel, whom I met then for the first time and who has remained a friend and client for over 50 years. After the war Cyril was *the* most in demand musical director in London. Rex Harrison would not sing without him, so of course he conducted *My Fair Lady* at Drury Lane. He was also the musical director for *Sunday Night at the London Palladium*, coping with the visiting American tops of the bill – not always easy. As a composer he wrote several hits, including 'Portrait of my Love', which almost everyone on both sides of the Atlantic recorded. His one successful musical, *Pickwick*, included of course the song which will always be associated with Harry Secombe – 'If I Ruled the World'. But the life of a composer is even more erratic than that of an actor, and romantic ballads went out of fashion. Nevertheless, Cyril has always been so grateful for the good times and in the lean times he has never once wavered in his loyalty.

My activities for a short time were to be centred on Hamburg. There was a report that two elephants had been found wandering in the area and had been captured. It led me on the trail of a circus. There was a strict order at the time against fraternisation with or employment of Germans.

Fortunately, dozens of artistes in northern Germany could claim to be 'displaced persons' and had, or quickly got hold of, papers to prove it. The elephants were part of Circus Belli. The Belli family were Latvians. We quickly gathered together as many of their animals and acts as we could find. The one thing Belli lacked was a big top. They told me that their rival, Hagenbach, had a big top and that he was an ardent Nazi. Whether this was true or not, I was by now too far down the line with Belli to care! I requisitioned the Hagenbach big top and handed it to my protégé. Years later, I heard that Hagenbach was in London enquiring, not too kindly, for 'that Major Stone'. Another quote:

> I'm worrying who are really Germans and who aren't and which we should employ – and Hagenbach is angry because I have taken his Big Top, which will seat two thousand troops! The circus is assuming fantastic proportions, eighty horses, two lions, and a monkey, fifty artistes and forty elephants. The Big Top oddly surmounted by two Union Jacks and two flags of Hamburg. We have swings and roundabouts and employ two hundred and fifty people.

We had an adventurous dress rehearsal for the new Circus Belli. The Old Vic, under the auspices of ENSA, were playing the Schauspielhaus theatre in Hamburg, now the Garrison Theatre. Olivier, Richardson, Sybil Thorndyke, Margaret Leighton and Joyce Redman sat in the audience. The circus orchestra, which was mounted on a bridge above the arch through which the animals made their entrance, began the overture. Lacking a conductor and being out of practice, the noise was horrendous. Ralph Richardson was concerned that the musicians were not getting enough to eat! It was too much for Herbert Menges, the Musical Director of the Old Vic. He climbed to the bridge and knocked the orchestra into shape. The circus was a huge success. We played three times daily for the troops. Soon they were allowed to give performances for the Germans. Belli could then charge admission, and so collected a little cash, as well as British rations which is all I had been able to contribute so far.

If, in those happy days, an officer wanted to fly, he went to the nearest RAF station and boarded the first plane going in the right direction. It was on a return trip from Brussels that Squadron Leader Cecil Landau and I were queuing as if for a London taxi. Cecil was later to produce those lavish revues *Sauce Tartare* and *Sauce Piquante* at the Cambridge Theatre and was to discover so much talent, including Audrey Hepburn, Bob Monkhouse and Norman Wisdom. He was a man of little patience. There was one seat left on the next Dakota flying to Luneburg. I was ahead of Cecil but he seemed in a hurry so I let him pass. His plane crash-landed in a field and Cecil was seriously hurt.

Having been promoted to major I was now allowed a staff captain. I hurried to a depot for unemployed officers to pick my man, but there was only one available. His name was George Brightwell. He admitted that he had no knowledge of show business, having been in insurance before the war. However, neither he nor I had any choice and so back he came. George enjoyed himself and remained in show business for the rest of his life in many capacities – not the least arduous of which was as manager and agent to Hughie Green.

Second Army disbanded, and the British Zone of Occupied Germany was divided into corps districts. I was posted to Thirty Corps as Entertainments Officer. I had the incredible good fortune to find myself serving once more under General Sir Brian Horrocks, who had been our corps commander in the desert. Horrocks was a charmer, which came across later in his fascinating television programmes. He was a splendid soldier, but an even more splendid man. I think he was pleased to find an old desert rat on his entertainments staff and sent for me. He made it clear that entertainment was now a top priority for an army with little to do and consisting mainly of wartime soldiers waiting for their demob. He wanted as much entertainment for the corps as possible. I asked if he was prepared to let me form a Thirty Corps Pool of Artistes, consisting of anyone in the corps with theatrical leaning regardless of rank. He agreed and sent out an order to that effect. My first applicant was Captain Ian Carmichael, whom I had only known by sight at RADA. He desperately wanted to act but I eventually persuaded him to become my staff captain, and so began a friendship for life and a long business association.

In 1945 we were both young and a little crazy and loved our world of Thirty Corps Entertainment. As a late riser, Ian was probably the only captain in the British Army who was brought his breakfast in bed by his immediate superior!

Our auditions were a success. Horrocks's 'regardless of rank' edict worked well. We formed the Thirty Corps Dance Band (with a full colonel playing third Trumpet and a lance corporal conducting), two concert parties, a repertory company and a string ensemble.

Frankie Howerd arrived driving a lorry. As we were just going to lunch, he asked if he could give an audition although not on the list. He gave it and I booked him, despite Ian thinking he was not funny at all. When a few months later he was due for demob, he asked me if I thought he should try his hand as a 'pro' in Civvy Street. I have always told the story very much against myself that the advice I gave him was 'no'. Some years ago Frankie, not the most secure of performers, asked me to lunch. I thought after 35 years, he was about to ask me to be his agent! This was not the case. He sat down with a longer face than usual. Was it true that I had been telling a story that, in 1945, I didn't consider him funny?

51

Even after I had assured him that it was a story only reflecting my own serious lack of judgement, he remained appalled. It turned out that in all the years, through his many ups and downs, he had consoled himself with the thought that there was one man at least in show business who believed in him. He then produced from his pocket a tired piece of army notepaper which he had cherished. It informed those whom it might concern that Corporal Howerd was a very funny man and was signed Richard Stone, Major!

I picked up Ian Carmichael's autobiography, *Will the Real Ian Carmichael...* He remembered it all so well:

My meeting with Richard Stone was to be the start of a very close relationship and personal friendship which was to last for twenty years.

[His book was written a while ago – we are still dear friends after 55 years.]

Richard was a driving force – that was and always has been his forte. The whole '30 Corps Theatrical Pool' project, as it eventually came to be known, was his. He was a human dynamo. Though good company, he was at times exhausting to be with. He lived and breathed his job and consequently assumed that all his minions did the same. He never relaxed; he was on the go the whole time. His plan was always the grand one, the broad strategy, and like so many other men with similar abilities he found it difficult to consider detail; that was for someone else to take care of – and for another year that someone was destined to be me.

Richard's own office was a small one. Beyond that was a larger room which resembled an amalgamation of the showrooms of Messrs Chappell, Boosey & Hawkes, the HMV record shop in Oxford Street and Frizell's, the Leicester Square chemist. Records, sheet music, musical instruments, make-up, copies of plays and sketches. All the time I knew that suite of offices it was never less populated than a department store on the first day of the January sales. If you wanted a letter traced you were in for trouble, but if you wanted the band parts of 'Someone's Rocking My Dreamboat' they were on your desk in a flash!

After about three months we had 30 shows on the road. The office itself was now permanently besieged by an endless stream of foreign artistes and their requirements. A conjuror who worked entirely on his own when we originally booked him suddenly acquired a girl assistant – no extra charge, but she would now qualify for British rations. Could we supply a permit for a new set of tyres for the Continental Express company coach – if not they could not possibly get to Wolfenbuttel to open next Monday. One female juggler actually arrived in the office one morning requesting that we should supply her with sanitary towels.

'Certainly dear, I always keep a handy supply in the bottom drawer of my desk.'

The saga of the circuses was a jolly little headache too. Apart from having to supply fodder for the horses and elephants, there was also a routing problem that reared its ugly head; Germany is a land of circuses, as we were very soon to find out.

We started out with one – Circus Althoff. For its opening fortnight we sent it to Osnabruck. On the first Wednesday morning the lady proprietor arrived in our office.

'Herr Kapitan,' she started, 'in Osnabruck this week is also Circus Heimsoth. It is not possible two circuses can do good business in one town. What you do for us, please?'

I apologised for the double booking but until her arrival, I explained, I had no knowledge of Circus Heimsoth's existence. Only one solution seemed possible. I got into a car and set off for Osnabruck. There I interviewed the proprietor of Circus Heimsoth and suggested that, in his own interests, maybe in future we should route his circus too, to avoid another clash. He readily agreed and in two weeks' time we sent Circus Heimsoth to Hanover and Circus Althoff to Hamelin.

On arriving in the office on Tuesday morning, Effi Plotz of Circus Althoff was waiting for me once again.

'Herr Kapitan,' she began dolefully, 'in Hamelin this week is Circus Charlie. Is not possible two circuses can do good business in Hamelin. What you do for us, please?'

Practically before she had finished, Herr Heimsoth also arrived in the office. 'Herr Kapitan. In Hanover this week is also Circus Bruckenbeck –' etc., etc., etc.

By the end of six weeks we were routing eight circuses. It was a nightmare. More elephants, more horses, more sea lions to feed. When I finally left Germany I prayed fervently that I should never see another circus as long as I lived.

ENSA put at our disposal a pool of actresses, who were housed in the town major's office in Nienburg. Ian and I were appearing in our spare moments with two of these girls. In *Springtime for Henry* Ian got off with the large-bosomed one and I was left with the skinny one, whom I didn't fancy. Ian sneaked off at night with his conquest. One snowy and freezing night, when the town major decided to make a round of inspection to see if his girls were comfortable, Ian had to make a typical farce exit onto the balcony and down the drainpipe in his underwear.

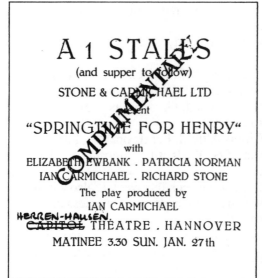

A 1 STALLS

(and supper to follow)

STONE & CARMICHAEL LTD

present

"SPRINGTIME FOR HENRY"

with

ELIZABETH EWBANK . PATRICIA NORMAN
IAN CARMICHAEL . RICHARD STONE

The play produced by
IAN CARMICHAEL

HERREN-HAUSEN.
CAPITOL THEATRE . HANNOVER

MATINEE 3.30 SUN. JAN. 27th

To get the best German artistes we needed to go to Berlin, where we used as agent Herr Wilk of the Scala. It was coming back on the autobahn, smuggling the artistes through the Russian Zone, that was tricky. In 3-ton lorries were the chorus girls, to whom it was explained that at the checkpoints at either end of the Russian Corridor they would have to lie down and be covered in sacking. The 'stars' were hidden in armoured cars. On one trip, they included a singing trio of redheads billed as the Three Sparrows and the entire cast of a show which we later called *Swelfare*. I wrote:

> They are the most delightful people and all big stars. I am a little embarrassed however by their great show of patriotism for Italy, Holland, China etc. when most of them have lived most of their lives in Germany. As Wilk of the Scala, who is a German and proud of it says, 'they didn't talk so much about their home countries during the war'.

We were asked by Brian Horrocks to arrange a cabaret of our best artistes for some special party at his headquarters. Captain James Ottaway, the actor, now also on our staff, Ian and I accompanied the performers, who included a glamorous cabaret singer Rosel Rauch. After a rather alcoholic evening, much against the advice of Jimmy and Ian, I accompanied Rosel to bed. It had been rumoured that whilst in Berlin, she had been Eisenhower's mistress, so I felt honoured.

Whilst on one of my trips to Berlin I wrote a rather extraordinary paragraph. It now seems quite far-fetched but I suppose it must be true:

> Russian soldiers will give up to two hundred pounds for any sort of watch, providing it is ticking. When it stops ticking they don't know how to wind it up and so change it for another. One Russian in a shop with an alarm clock wanted it made into three small ones! Another

had an alarm tied round his neck and when it went off he threw it in the gutter and shot it.

It is quite interesting, in view of how soon ENSA was to pack up and that I was to take over that I wrote the following:

Basil Dean was around the other day. The General won't see him on principal. He is even a laughing stock to his own staff now. Quite a number of ENSA shows are unplayable, I wonder what will happen to him.

Felix De Wolfe was by now the Entertainments Officer for the RAF Group in the Thirty Corps zone and we had monthly meetings. It was at one of these meetings that we decided to go into partnership as agents when we were demobbed. I had been enjoying so much the administration and organisation of my show business army that I had, with a certain sadness, decided that my talents might be better employed as an agent and impresario than by returning to be a performer.

On 31st October, our eldest son, Barry, was born at Kings College Hospital. A distinguished visitor was Robert Donat, who came with a view to Sara playing Cinderella in *The Glass Slipper*. He offered Sara the part and rehearsals began the day she left hospital. A nanny was found who wheeled Barry each day at feeding time from Ebury Street to the St James Theatre, and from the dress circle, the beautiful voice of Robert Donat told the company, 'There will now be a twenty-minute break whilst Cinderella feeds the baby!' By now Donat was a sick man. The days of his greatest films – *Inn of the Sixth Happiness*, *Goodbye Mr Chips* were past. He suffered terribly from asthma and was making a few stage appearances, but working mostly as an impresario.

My date for repatriation to England and demobilisation approached. I wrote to Sara:

This is the last letter I shall ever write to you because war has parted us. I am coming home tomorrow week. We shall be together for always. There have been lonely wretched moments when I wanted you by my side – and these will never come again.

On arrival in England I was sent for by John Leather, the adjutant of my training regiment. The meeting was to change my plans for the next few years. John was now in Welfare, in charge of army entertainment worldwide. ENSA was to be disbanded, and in its place was to be set up a service organisation to provide live entertainment for the army, navy and air force.

55

John asked if I would be interested to delay my demob and become its first chief with the rank of lieutenant colonel? Having enjoyed my time running Thirty Corps Entertainment, the idea of running the whole shooting match was very appealing, but I had already agreed to set up an agency with Felix. My father had provided the necessary starting capital of £1,000, and Felix's father had curtained off a small space at the back of De Wolfe Music at 80 Wardour Street for our first offices. With some trepidation I asked John if I could have it both ways. Proceeding with my demob, could I be given, as a civilian, the honorary rank of lieutenant colonel and wear uniform on suitable occasions? And could I be allowed to continue the setting up of the De Wolfe and Stone Agency? Incredibly the answer to both questions was yes.

We christened the new outfit Combined Services Entertainment, and it is still functioning today. There were still large occupying armies from Europe through the Middle East to India and Singapore, all gasping for entertainment. Basil Dean was not much loved but at least he was a considerable figure in the theatrical world, and who was going to replace him? A 26-year-old soldier, masquerading as a colonel, with a year's experience as an actor before the war, and absolutely no right to give birth to such an important baby! But the baby stumbled, walked and then ran.

My first hazard was an officer appointed by the RAF to look after their interests and to be my second in command. Flight Lieutenant Roy Cowl looked as shifty as he was. He had run a concert party, Roy Cowl's Queeries, before the war and by 1946 was a balding, Telly Savalas-like figure who had been supervising air force shows. He knew all the variety agents in the Charing Cross Road, and frankly was more than a match for his young boss. After about six months when I was on a tour of inspection in Singapore, John Leather caught him doling out some contracts with built-in percentages payable to Roy Cowl, and he was sacked. He was last heard of some 20 years later leaving a theatrical company stranded in Lyme Regis.

In the main we worked through some of the smaller play and revue producers. On the variety side I stumbled across one John D. Roberton, a bluff North Country revue proprietor whose productions included *We Were in the Forces*, *Nine O'Clock Nudes*, *Naughty but Nice* and *The Lamp that was Blue*.

For between £100 and £200 John provided a complete revue consisting of a principal comedian, his 'feed', two or three acts, dancers, singers and a chorus of 12, plus scenery and costumes. God knows what salary he paid the chorus girls. With an engagement abroad, a uniform, officer status and 'all found', they probably paid him!

His two young sons Bill and Jack were usually employed as 'feed' and company manager. Bill Roberton later worked in my office for many years

56

producing summer shows. Jack, taking the surname of Douglas, became first of all part of a double act, Baker and Douglas, and then a regular member of the 'Carry On' team.

The artistes for smaller shows were booked direct and Ian Carmichael, who had since been demobbed, was brought in to produce revues. There was a little forces club just off the Strand with a minute stage, called the Nuffield Centre. Twice a week there were free concerts for the troops, where young ex-service artistes did their turns. Sitting in a small enclosed room at the back and above the hall were the agents, managers and bookers, talent spotting. Some of the ex-service artistes who had been great favourites in the army were not so lucky in Civvy Street. Norman Caley, 'The Mad Earl' had been a riot in the Middle East, so had Jack 'Shufty Allatoola' Anton. They both survived, but only just. More fortunate was Marty Feldman, whom I personally found totally unfunny and told to give it up! Harry Secombe, sang like an angel but his attempts at comedy then were faltering. Spike Milligan as zany as ever, and Bob Monkhouse as confident then as now! Ian Carmichael and I visited the Nuffield Centre, music halls and nightclubs almost every night. At the Eve Club Ian spotted a magician and told me to book him. It was Ian who pointed out to him the humour of getting his tricks wrong and helped foster the genius of Tommy Cooper.

My efforts were not appreciated by the comedian Wee Georgie Wood, who considered that some of the variety acts, especially himself, who regularly played the number one music hall circuit, Moss Empires, were being ignored by CSE. In his weekly column in *The Stage* newspaper he asked 'Who is this rolling Stone who gathers no Moss Acts?'

One of our most popular shows was built around Ivy Benson and her all girls band, and included the Beverley Twins before they joined up with the third sister, who is actually a cousin! The lucky man in this outfit was Hugh Lloyd. He will forgive my saying that his success as an actor makes up for his lack of promise as a stand-up comic!

Although in honour bound not to put any business the way of De Wolfe and Stone, my time in CSE was not wasted as I made useful contacts for the future. 'Stars in Battledress' came under CSE and both Benny Hill and Reg Varney came to the office after first meeting me as their colonel. Touring the world, it was in Singapore that I saw Reg Varney. There are some quotes from letters I wrote on this trip that are a happy reminder of leisurely, luxury air travel, sadly a thing of the past.

We left Poole this morning. It's a Sunderland Flying Boat. I am in the lounge cabin with a General and his ADC, a Brigadier, and an English and Dutch civilian. There are the most wonderful armchairs. We spend most of the time eating. Lunch was soup, cold sole and salad, chicken, heavenly ice cream, cheese and coffee. We keep popping down to refuel, first at Marseilles, then at Augusta in Sicily, then in Cairo. We shall be in Singapore about midday on Sunday.

Further stops on the way to Singapore were Basra and Karachi. And on the way back:

Yesterday, Saturday, I got on a 'C' class Flying Boat for Cairo. This is even larger than a Sunderland, has about twenty-five armchairs, each with its own table etc. It's a shuttle service stopping five times between Karachi and Cairo and taking two days.

Wisely, I do not seem to have written admitting to enjoying the charms of one of my leading ladies in Shepheard's Hotel!

On a trip to Germany I first saw Benny Hill. Benny was the driver and second comedian of a 'Stars in Battledress' show starring a comedian Sergeant Harry Segal. The local officer who had replaced me, one Bill Day, after seeing a dress rehearsal in Nienburg of Sergeant Segal's show, cut out Private Hill's act, which he thought unfunny. A few days later the show was playing in the beautiful miniature opera house in the castle at Celle. Harry Segal knew that the Colonel was in front and re-instated Benny's turn. Benny was great and I told him so. Our paths were to cross soon after his demob, and I was his agent for 40-odd years. One of his favourite lines was 'I've got the Colonel working for me now!'

But the Benny Hill/Bill Day saga had a good ending. Some years later Bill was managing a pub in the New Forest. He had arranged a dance for New Year's Eve and needed a cabaret. To repay him for thinking he was unfunny in Germany, Bill rang me to book Benny, whose fee for a night was then £30. When Benny arrived the dance had failed to attract and was cancelled. Bill gave Benny his cheque. Benny forgot to cash it and months later was walking down the Charing Cross Road, where he bumped into Harry Segal. Benny asked how things were going and Harry told him that he had an offer for pantomime but had to provide his own costumes, which he couldn't afford. As the costumes would cost about £30, Benny gave Harry Bill's cheque and all concerned had paid their debts!

In 1947 we moved to our first reasonable home, a picturesque cottage behind a terrace of houses in Manchester Street. My year at CSE was up. John asked me to extend and, audaciously, I demanded to work mornings for CSE and afternoons for De Wolfe and Stone. I stayed on for another year!

7

Reg Varney and Sara, our biggest earners, Benny Hill booked as Reg's stooge after beating Peter Sellers at an audition. Billing problems with Terry Scott and Jimmy Logan and Shirley Eaton in Goldfinger

And so in 1947 I divided my time between CSE in Eaton Square and the De Wolfe and Stone offices in the curtained-off area behind De Wolfe Music in Wardour Street. I am often asked 'What does a theatrical agent do exactly?'

Is an agent the much caricatured fast-talking, chain cigar-smoking combination of Fagin and Uriah Heep? Is he the one who, watching the trapeze artistes in the circus flying through the air risking life and limb, shouts 'There go the bastards who are taking ninety per cent of my salary'?

Or is it he walking with his partner down Charing Cross Road commiserating on the death of a more successful colleague who asks, 'What do you think he left, Joe?' And Joe replies, 'Max Miller, Gert and Daisy, Marquis the Chimp and the Dagenham Girl Pipers.'

Is it true that God, testing three candidates for entry to heaven, asked the first two what professions they had followed. One replied that he was a doctor, the other a schoolmaster. So God asked them to pass a simple spelling test. He asked them to spell 'France' and, finding the third candidate was a theatrical agent, he asked him to spell Czechoslovakia! Did one actor put a codicil in his will that he was to be cremated and ten per cent of his ashes were to be thrown over his agent? And did another actor, returning home after his show one evening to find his wife bruised, beaten up and raped ask her who on earth did it, and when she gasped through her tears that it was his agent, did he ask her, 'Did he leave any message for me?'

Agents come in all shapes and sizes. They range from the no-hoper with the stuttering ventriloquist and the one-armed juggler, so brilliantly immortalised by Woody Allen in the film *Broadway Danny Rose*, to the quiet English, gentlemanly, dignified, Laurie Evans, who has represented Olivier, Gielgud, Guinness, Richardson and most of the titled aristocracy of the British theatre. At the top of the market a lot of agents prefer to be called personal managers, and for their 10, 12½ or 15 per cent of everything their clients earn look after a limited number of artistes on an exclusive basis.

With beginners and unknowns that job is recommending them to producers, directors and casting directors, and thereby fixing them work — any work. The actor Geoffrey Hughes, so brilliant as Onslow in *Keeping Up Appearances*, says that with Richard Stone, you are not often out of work. If there's nothing better going, 'You find yourself juggling canaries at the end of Southend pier'! As the artiste begins to climb the ladder the task becomes more creative. The agent still has to find work for the client but he has to make sure that it is the right work. If there are two jobs on offer, one to star in a bad horror movie for £1,000 a week, and the other to join the Royal Shakespeare Company for £250 a week, it may be the agent who has to persuade the client to take the second job. It can be hard for an actor to take the long-term view if he is broke and has a wife and two children to support. When and if the artiste reaches the top, then the agent can sit back a bit and wait for the phone to ring. The actor is now a 'star' or a 'draw' and the agent's role is to read scripts on offer, sort out the best job available and do a good deal with the producer.

What is a star? A star is magical. A star puts bums on seats over a period of years. A draw, on the other hand, is an artiste who, temporarily boosted by playing a running character in a television series, puts bums on seats this year, but next year, who knows? I find it quite ludicrous that today everyone in the cast is a star. Journalists, after naming the one and only real star in a film or play, then go rambling on with 'the show also stars . . .' and list the cast of totally adequate but unknown actors. I even recently read of a pantomime that 'also starred' the babes from the local dancing school!

Once satisfied that he has got the best financial deal possible, the artiste starts worrying about 'the billing', the bane of most agents' lives. Billing to an actor assumes the importance of the third world war, and it seems to his agent that hostilities are about to commence with each new contract. Such concern must be incomprehensible to the general public, referred to in the Green Room Club as the 'punters'.

So let me explain. The billing clause in a contract determines the position, the size and often the colour of the artiste's name. It also spells out how and where this applies. For instance, on a film it may only be guaranteed on the screen itself, the theory being that once a film is released the producer has little control over a cinema manager in, say, Hong Kong. Mr Woo may choose to bill the local beauty queen playing

60

one scene in preference to the 20 international stars whose agents have fought so hard to get them placed in an agreed pecking order. There was an amusing incident concerning billing early in my career. Shirley Eaton was the much publicised golden girl of an early James Bond film, *Goldfinger*. I arranged, with Harry Saltzman, the producer, a special billing clause for Shirley. It stated that she would be billed on the screen and in all publicity under the control of the producer in a certain size with the words 'Introducing Shirley Eaton'. On the day of the opening, this being my first decent film deal, I was drawn to Leicester Square hopefully to see her name in large type. In fact there was no trace of Shirley's name outside the Odeon Leicester Square. I phoned my solicitor and together we took photographs. Harry Saltzman could have claimed that the Rank Organisation, who owned the Odeon, were to blame, and that it was 'not under his control', but this soon became academic. When the film opened, it transpired that they had also forgotten the screen credit! Shirley was very upset. It was a genuine oversight and Harry was most apologetic. But we had a contract. It would have been a very expensive job, entailing re-editing the entire opening sequence. We reached a compromise and Harry paid Shirley a large sum of money to swallow her pride and cry all the way to the bank. The compensation was far in excess of the fee she had been paid for the entire film, including the discomfort of being painted in the nude in gold!

Billing establishes the pecking order in the theatre for many things. Dressing rooms for instance are allocated according to billing. In the line-up at the end of the show when the artistes are acknowledging, so modestly, your applause, they are in the billing order, working outwards from the star, who stands in the centre. The more insecure the artistes the more they care about the billing. In the late 1940s, I booked two clients for a year's tour in Ivor Novello's *Perchance to Dream*. Sylvia Cecil was then an ageing and disgruntled leading lady. John McHugh was a wild Irish tenor who had made a small reputation on radio and records. They were to be billed side by side, exactly equal, Sylvia Cecil on the left, John McHugh on the right. They weren't exactly best of friends and the management *never* got the billing right. Every Monday for 40-odd weeks there would be a call to me from one or the other. From Southsea, Sylvia would call to say that John McHugh was billed first on the local trams and the next week John would call from Cardiff to say that he was not billed at all on any of the buses!

Julian Orchard, he of the long lugubrious face, was not normally concerned about billing, until one year, when perhaps already suffering from the cancer from which he so sadly died, he hit the roof. He was billed to appear in pantomime at Richmond, enacting his gloriously funny ugly sister with Melvyn Hayes. The first five names on the bill were repre-

61

sented by my office and were meant to be of equal size, with Julian in third position. Through some misunderstanding in the management's office, Bill Pertwee was promoted to third position. Dear Julian went mad. He had been at the London Palladium the previous year with Terry Scott and received third billing. He couldn't tolerate coming to Richmond and being fourth, and was most concerned what his friends would think, especially as he lived locally.

Perhaps his friends would have been surprised to learn how much it meant to him, and even more surprised if they had known that, as it was partly my fault, I paid the management £1,000 to re-do all the printing in the correct order!

Talking of Terry Scott reminds me of another funny billing situation. Jimmy Logan was a big pantomime star in Scotland, but one year the city of Edinburgh decided that they would like a co-star for Jimmy from England for their pantomime. I stupidly suggested Terry Scott, forgetting that Jimmy and Terry, both clients and both normally very easy to deal with, had been together before and hadn't exactly hit it off. The first of many problems was the billing. Jimmy Logan had always had first billing in Scotland, Terry Scott had always had it in England. So I arranged that Terry Scott was to be billed on the left with his picture and that Jimmy Logan, with his picture, was to be on the right, but higher up the poster. This simple artifice hopefully deluded both contestants that they had won the battle! It was spelt out on both contracts, with added clauses that their photographs must be included on all advertising. The pay-off was a call from a lugubrious entertainments executive for the Edinburgh council. He planned to put an advertisement in the trade paper *The Stage* for chorus girls. He thought it would look impressive if he let them know it was for the Terry Scott/Jimmy Logan pantomime. He was ringing to ask if he had to put both their pictures in the advertisement. As Terry was in South Africa and Jimmy in Australia at the time, we let it go!

In the variety world emphasis can sometimes be given by surrounding the artiste's name with a box. 'For God's sake,' you tell the management, 'put him in a box' and often you mean it! When the billing has finally been agreed and the show is on the road, then the artiste rings the agent to complain about the lack of publicity. Every agent representing a dubious star name who is emptying a provincial theatre has had to listen to the complaint that he or she is playing to empty houses because there aren't any posters in the town. And then comes the classic line: 'I was in Marks and Spencer and a lady came up and said, "Aren't you Arthur Crabtree? What are you doing in Scunthorpe, on holiday, are you?"'

The truth is that the public, if they really want to see an artiste, will find him, even if he's playing in an unmarked tent on Salisbury Plain.

In America almost all actors have a manager as well as an agent, and so pay away sometimes as much as half their earnings. It seldom happens in England but when it does, in my experience it's a disaster. The manager, trying to prove himself, whispers into the actor's ear disparaging remarks about the poor agent and queries all the deals he tries to make. Worse is the amateur manager, usually a husband, wife or lover. And worst of all is the husband, wife or lover on the fringe of the business who knows it all.

I was very fond of Wendy Craig and of her husband Jack Bentley, an excellent show business writer. But Jack knew about every show going into production, and some that weren't, and quite unwittingly made my life hell. He adored Wendy, and if he heard that there was a film possibly going to be made, if they could get the rights and if they could find the money, on say the life of Marlene Dietrich, Jack would want to know if I'd submitted Wendy to play Marlene, despite the fact she couldn't sing, was an English rose, and anyway was tied to television for the next two years.

Ruth Madoc's husband was worse because he knew nothing. One day he was a trumpeter in the army; Ruth fell for him, they got married and the next day he was Mr Show Business.

Worst of all was a girl call Susan Hanson, who was one of the leads in *Crossroads*. She came to me because she wanted to play in pantomime and I fixed her with my friend Paul Elliot at an outrageously high salary to play Cinderella at Southsea. Just before rehearsals started I got a call from her husband, the singer Carl Wayne.

'I'm her manager and she won't do the pantomime.'

I exploded into the phone. 'I never knew she had a manager. She either goes to Southsea or leaves my office.'

She did the pantomime.

De Wolfe and Stone were now established above a gunsmith's in William IV Street opposite the old Charing Cross Hospital. We had acquired a good stable of artistes, but Sara, co-starring with Bruce Trent in *Goodnight Vienna* on a long tour for Bernard Delfont, was our biggest earner at £75 a week. She was also the only client from whom I earned 95 per cent! We had taken her over from the Lionel Wallace Agency. Lionel Wallace specialised in pantomime artistes. Interviewing a young hopeful he would smile wistfully, offering her chorus, then he would pinch her cheek, fondle her boobs, and put his hand between her legs, offering her with each descent first fairy, and then principal girl and finally principal boy.

It was at Lewisham that Eric Maschwitz, its author, happening to be passing the theatre, asked the manager how *Goodnight Vienna* was doing in Lewisham. His classic reply was, 'Just about as well as *Goodnight Lewisham* would do in Vienna.'

During this tour Sara was carrying our second son, Tim. One matinee making her grand entrance she tripped at the top of a long flight of stairs and rolled to the bottom. Tim took it in his stride!

One of our first clients was the late Anthony Sharp. He had a small but effective part in *Who Goes There*, which was being tried out at Windsor Rep. The play, and its very young leading lady, Geraldine McEwan, caught the eye of the enormous impresario Henry Sherek. During the war Henry had served in a smart regiment, married a titled lady, and became a great military and social snob. He rang me to book Tony for the transfer of the show to London and was at great pains to point out that it was a small part and that it would be Mr Sharp's first chance in the West End. He offered a salary of £27 10s. I pointed out that Tony Sharp had been a major in the Royal Horse Artillery. 'Oh well in that case, make it thirty-five pounds.'

Fortunately the agency business in England is not dominated by large corporations as it is in America. We are a small band of London agents each with a star or more and a stable of distinguished actors. When a star's career begins to wane, they either sit it out or blame the agent and move to one of our colleagues, who then has a hard task. Take as an example Barbara Windsor. She was discovered by Peter Charlesworth as a teenager and he cleverly guided her career until she reached the top. She adored Peter but when there was a lull in her career she left him and came to me. Now the irony is that I had the hard job and the difficult times, what with Ronnie Knight in jail and Barbara not at all in demand. In a recent interview on TV she talked of the time when all she could get was pantomime and summer season. Darling Barbara, you will never know how hard I had to work to get you those pantomimes and summer seasons. I packaged plays, I put on tours, I even put up the money to produce a little show called *Carry on Barbara* and persuaded a friendly impresario to take it to New Zealand, where it emptied the theatres. Now Barbara is a national treasure and back on top once more.

At Combined Services Entertainments, I had been earning a colonel's salary of about £30 a week, and the profits of De Wolfe and Stone had yielded roughly the same amount, which in fairness all went to Felix. Now we had to double our profits to maintain our basic standard of living. Felix and I used to come in on Saturday mornings to enter up the commission for the week, which fortunately began to improve.

Another early client was Anthony Hayes. Tony had been Jack Hulbert's understudy before the war. When Jack selected him at an audition he was concerned that the new man, although very good, if he ever had to play for him, might look a little young opposite Cis. Cis chipped in that in that case she would go to bed early and Tony must stay up all night! In 1950, I had booked Tony in a provincial pantomime when he was offered the lead in *The Boy Friend* at the Players Theatre underneath the arches in Charing Cross. He begged me to get him released from Alderman Fitzwarren to

FELIX DE WOLFE and RICHARD STONE

(Licensed Annually by the L.C.C.)

4/5, William IV Street, London, W.C.2

January, 1950   Temple Bar 2112/3/4

Representing Musical Artistes :

(This list is issued in conjunction with our full list of contract artistes, for easy reference of managements and agents dealing in musical-comedy, revue and variety).

COMEDIANS

JACK ANTON

GEORGE BENSON

WALLAS EATON

RICHARD GILBERT

VIC GORDON & PETER COLVILLE

BENNY HILL

*EDDIE MOLLOY

REG VARNEY

PRODUCTION ARTISTES

IAN CARMICHAEL

KENNETH CONNOR

DAVID DAVIES (Baritone)

WILLIAM DICKIE (Baritone)

GAVIN GORDON (Bass Baritone)

ANTHONY HAYES

JOHN McHUGH (Tenor)

HUGH MORTON

NIGEL NEILSON (Light Baritone)

BILL O'CONNOR (Tenor)

IVAN STAFF

IAN WALLACE (Bass Baritone)

PRODUCTION ARTISTES

DAPHNE ANDERSON

MAI BACON

IRENE EISINGER (Soprano)

LINDA GRAY (Mezzo-Soprano)

SARA GREGORY (Soprano)

*DORIS HARE

ROSE HILL (Soprano)

HATTIE JACQUES

GAIL KENDAL

STELLA MORAY

* Not represented for variety

65

accept the Players. I pointed out the apparent stupidity of turning his back on £30 a week for a long run in favour of £8 a week for a very short run in a very doubtful starter. But Tony had faith. I got him released on the understanding that he would fulfil the pantomime engagement as soon as he was free. Eight years later, when he finished the post-London tour of *The Boy Friend*, the pantomime promoter was dead. I used to love Harold Hobson's annual remark in the *Sunday Times*: 'But the best performance in a musical in London is still Anthony Hayes in *The Boy Friend*.' And when it was revived, years later, Hobson wrote: 'But there will never be another Anthony Hayes.'

Dear Tony is dead now, but the day before he died he was tapping away and singing 'I could be happy with you'.

Reg Varney was the first of my comedians to earn good money. Reg had a strong stage act which included playing the accordion and piano very well. He was so important to me that I went with him to the Dorchester Hotel, where he was booked for a private gig, and carried his accordion through the kitchens of the hotel to the banqueting room! He was appearing in a chi-chi revue, *Billy Milton's Party*, at the St James Theatre, when he was spotted by the concert party proprietor Hedley Claxton, whose shows all round the coast were innocently called *Gaytime*. It was because Hedley wanted a feed for Reg that Benny Hill and I got together again after the war. We went to see him at the Kilburn Empire, but he still had to audition. Peter Sellers was at the same audition, but Benny got the job. Peter, before becoming an international film star, was a very indifferent impressionist, and strangely had little or no personality as himself.

Benny has been called the most famous comedian in the world, and since his breakthrough in America and the sale of his shows to over 90 countries, it is undoubtedly true. But when Reg Varney was getting his £75 a week and a percentage, I booked Benny into the same show for £16 a week, and for this he did his act, was straight man to Reg and company manager! It was a miracle we stayed together so many years, Benny and I. For, of all the artistes I looked after in those days, I confess I failed to realise that Benny had the greatest potential of them all. I was so keen on Reg Varney.

I had a pre-war Morris 8 in which I drove all the pantomime and variety bookers to Cliftonville to see my star, perhaps casually mentioning during the evening that I also represented the young second comic, Benny Hill. Years later, when Benny became the first comedy star created by television, Reg Varney left the office. I don't know if it was jealousy or because he thought, quite erroneously, that I was ignoring him for Benny. Reg would never have been more than a good reliable middle-of-the-road variety artist. But as a comedy actor, of course, he had a great career in *The Rag Trade* and *On The Buses*.

66

Benny played several summer seasons for Hedley. At the end of each one, Hedley Claxton gave him a keyring in recognition of his company management.

Benny and Reg were booked to go on tour for George and Alfred Black, in a number two revue. A number one revue with either the London star or a big provincial name would play the prestigious Moss empire and Stoll circuits. A number two revue would play all the crummier dates from the Camberwell Palace to West Hartlepool. There was a sketch that Reg particularly wanted to include from their summer show, but George and Alf wanted to see it first. I managed to book 'Reg Varney and company' for a Saturday night at the town hall, Poplar, through the booking agent for £50. I assembled a cast of five and offered them each £10, which they were more than eager to earn. The 'boxers' were Reg Varney and Benny Hill, the 'seconds' Ian Wallace and Philip Dale, and the referee Ian Carmichael! We rehearsed on the Saturday morning, in De Wolfe and Stone's office, and duly completed the engagement. George and Alf liked the sketch and I paid out the £10 each, but unfortunately the cheque from the booking agent made out to me bounced and I am still £50 short.

In the tough northern dates Benny's act was dying a horrible death. The local theatre managers were complaining in droves. George and Alfred were sorry – they personally liked Benny's work but his act would have to go. Benny could stay and feed Reg at the same money, or leave the show. I cannot remember what advice I gave Benny, but given my track record with him so far, it was probably wrong! Anyway *he* decided to leave. He was out of work for six months and it was the turning point in his career. He started to appear in variety shows for the BBC. There were occasional television shows from the Nuffield Centre introduced by Richard Murdoch. Once, at short notice, Richard was ill and Benny was booked to compere the show. More Nuffield shows were followed by his own show live from the Television Centre.

By now Benny was a minor star. He toured in variety, with Teddy Johnson as first star, Benny Hill second and Pearl Carr third. Soon he was booked for his own twice-nightly show. I remember the salary offered was £125 a week. But, by now, I too had grown more experienced and I settled for £100 a week and a percentage. The show played to enormous business and Benny earned several hundred a week. Further stage shows followed but his last major stage appearance was at the Palace Theatre, Shaftesbury Avenue, in 1959, in a revue called *Fine Fettle*, which he wrote himself.

Benny never liked working in the theatre. He suffered with nerves, but most of all I think he hated the monotony of doing the same thing night after night. From that day on he concentrated entirely on television, with a few excursions to foreign parts to make the odd commercial.

67

Benny certainly was a loner. Although he talked a lot about the 'glorious birds' that he had been entertaining, if I ever dropped into his flat announced or unannounced, I found him alone, working at scripts, frying himself some supper. He didn't have a car or a servant and spent most of his leisure time on the Continent (especially in his beloved Camargue) wandering, writing, and observing other comedians, and particularly circus clowns.

He did his own shopping and often came back from the supermarket with a load of tins that the labels had fallen off. They were cheap, and exciting to open! He wrote his scripts on the backs of envelopes and scruffy bits of paper and posted them to Dennis Kirkland, his director, from all over Europe. He was probably closer to Dennis than anyone, except his mother.

Benny spent time in Felixstowe, looking after a disabled woman. He was not part of the show business scene. One well-known impresario said that, either he didn't exist at all, or I kept him in a cupboard and brought him out to make shows! He was my most enigmatic client. I knew him not very well for 40 years. He called me Squire.

In the early days we spent some leisure time together. One time he joined Sara and me in Paris. He was a conventional tourist. He showed us round Montmartre, took us to the Eiffel Tower, and on his favourite outing in a bateau mouche. Later this camaraderie waned but I think he respected me still.

He didn't really care about money and carried cheques for thousands of pounds in his pocket, forgetting for months to pay them in. He had no idea of his wealth. His money was invested for him, and well. Despite this, at one stage he became desperately worried that he was being cheated because the senior partner of the international firm of accountants who looked after his money was seen at the races! He was also suspicious of my dealings with his boss at Thames, the Head of Light Entertainment, Philip Jones, because we went fishing together. In fact my friendship with Philip ensured the best twenty years of Benny's career, without a single dispute of any kind. But Benny thought, quite wrongly, that I was working for the enemy.

For those who worked under him he had great affection. His cast included Henry McGee, Bob Todd (who was often so drunk that he could barely stand let alone remember lines), Jackie Wright, and particularly dear Sue Upton, whose kids he adored, and who was still a 'Hill's Angel' way past the normal age for dancers.

I attended almost every one of his shows at Thames for 20 years. He worried if I didn't turn up. I would watch the run-throughs, give him a couple of notes and watch the recording. After, I would go straight to his dressing room and without joining the others in the bar, we would gather up his bits and pieces and I would drive him back to his flat in Queen's Gate. Never in all those years did he ask me in for a drink or a coffee!

Although he was in demand in America he didn't want to go there. He turned down all the offers that were made and then complained that we hadn't got him any. From time to time he wrote me vitriolic letters claiming that our association was a disaster. I received those letters usually when he was unhappy within himself and was using me to let off steam.

He had one great friend, the agent Peter Charlesworth. I feared that after one of these outbursts he would leave me and go to Peter. But Peter was his chum, and I was his guvnor and soon all was forgotten. It was a tricky ride but he remained loyal to the end.

I thought of an amusing incident tied up with Barbara Windsor which should have been on page 64 but it was too late, the book was ready to go to press. My kind publishers, however, said it would fit in here.

When I was looking after Barbara, I also had Liz Fraser. If Barbara was having a bad time, Liz was doing worse and was, in the nicest way, a bit jealous even of Barbara's pantomimes and summer seasons! I booked Barbara to star in some rather tatty tour but she fell ill and was replaced by Liz. I made sure that, with only a few days' notice, all the posters were reprinted. Liz sent me a telegram, 'Business disastrous. Should have been billed as Barbara Windsor.'

8

*Summer shows on Clacton Pier, Dave Allen,
Harry Secombe – and dealing with Billy Butlin, Bernie
Delfont and the Grades*

In 1948 I began presenting summer shows, and this double life as a seaside impresario and agent was to continue for over 20 years. I fell in love with concert party in 1939 at Saltburn, and indeed had it not been for the war would have been the light comedian in *Twinkle*! Summer shows before the war and for at least a decade after were a gentlemanly affair. The impresarios were in the main a husband and wife team who both appeared in their own shows. There were as well as Clarkson Rose and Olive Fox in *Twinkle*, Cyril Fletcher and Betty Astell in *The Magpies*, John Berryman and Adele Wessely in *Evening Stars* and Ronnie and Dickie Brandon in *Out of the Blue*. The boss was usually the principal comedian and his lady the comedienne or character woman. Olive Fox and Adele Wessely were not particularly talented but, as the bosses' wives, were free labour. They found difficulty in finding material for an obligatory turn in each programme and I vividly remember them both sitting in front of a mock-up dressing-room table making up, awaiting the call-boy, and reciting a mawkish monologue regretting the end of a career entitled 'Last Beginners Please'. Sitting in the audience I, for one, prayed that soon make-believe would become reality. Betty Astell, who was a soprano and, being also in charge of the wardrobe, saw to it that she lived up to her billing as 'The Girl in the Crinoline Gown'! There were sometimes six programmes changed every Tuesday and Thursday on the doubtful assumption that a holidaymaker on a two-week vacation would visit the show four times, and if tempted to stay an extra week would come again, and twice! The young comedians tried out new material in front of a relaxed and happy audience and learnt to entertain and charm. Today's comedians are bred in pubs and clubs and it's difficult for them not to become hard.

Harry Secombe perfected his 'shaving act' in Cyril Fletcher's *Magpies*. Leslie Crowther was a member of the Fol-de-Rols, a team show with brilliant original material by its owner, Greatrix Newman. Benny and Reg were in *Gaytime*, but it was Ronnie and Dickie Brandon who had the best nose for comedy. When I first met them Norman Wisdom and David Nixon were in *Out of the Blue* – Terry Scott and Hugh Lloyd were to follow, but their favourite was Roy Hudd. I'm certain it was his many years with them that made Roy Hudd the wonderful all-rounder that he is today. Dickie was a dancer and featured herself in dramatic ballets, in one of which – the *Nun's Ballet* – she lost a foot. Norman, Terry and Roy found this a hard act to follow with laughs. One of the lovely things about these family summer shows was the business etiquette. There were as many good dates as good shows. It was the custom not to 'poach'. Until it was known that Cyril Fletcher was moving on from, say, Torquay, the others would not think of applying for the date – 'After you, Cyril!'

'End of the pier comedy' has become a sneering catch-phrase of high-brow critics. I couldn't have started any further down the pier. At the end of Clacton Pier, perched high above the slot machines, sits the Jolly Roger. At the shore end of the pier was the Ocean Theatre, and here there was a grand summer show with scenery and costumes and 12 chorus girls, featuring an unknown Tony Hancock. *The Ocean Revue* was produced by Frank Adey, with whom we had become friendly. Mrs Kingsman, who owned the pier, wanted him to book a small concert party for the Jolly Roger, and Frank offered me the contract at £100 a week on account of 50 per cent of the takings. With admission prices, of 3s, 2s and 1s, this could bring my share up to £200 a week if we filled the hall. I had no capital in 1948, so I was determined to break even on my £100 a week. I paid a double act, Gordon and Colville, both just out of the forces, £20 a week joint. A pianist and four other artistes cost £55. This left me £25 a week, out of which I must pay for costumes, some token scenery, royalties and rehearsal costs. We came in on budget! I even persuaded Horrocks, a company who made cotton dresses until they went broke the following year, to give us several dresses for the girls free, in exchange for a full-page credit in the programme. I paid Ian Carmichael £30 to produce the two pro-grammes. (This was, at the time, not bad for Ian. In *She Wanted a Cream Front Door* in London, he had been paid £11 a week by Blanche Littler, wife of George Robey, 'The Prime Minister of Mirth'. When the show went on tour, Blanche suggested that as Ian's part was only in the third act and his costume was a dinner jacket, he could well double as front of house and business manager. Under these circumstances she would not have to ask him to reduce his £11 a week salary!)

David Croft was the other member of the staff. Now, over 50 years later, he is known as the renowned writer and director of *Dad's Army* and a string of other TV series. Then he was a struggling actor and a BBC Show Band singer. I paid him £10 to collect the costumes and props and to acquire the scenery, which consisted then, and for most of our early shows, of a piece of garden trellis decorated with a few artificial flowers. I had not booked the pianist by the time the posters had to be printed, so we invented the name 'Eddie Clinton'. Hopefully the distinguished musician William Blezzard has forgiven me his billing that year in Clacton!

The Lagoon Follies were to be on once nightly at 8.15 p.m. At 8 o'clock on the opening night, Felix and I were sitting in two deck chairs on the prom anxiously looking down at the box office and counting the potential customers. We need not have worried. It soon became obvious why we were starting 15 minutes later than *The Ocean Revue*. Frank Adey appeared with a hand-held megaphone shouting '*Ocean Revue* now full — plenty of room in the Jolly Roger!'

And we sold out every house for the season on the overflow and made a £1,000 profit on my first ever summer show.

I was not the only one starting out on Clacton Pier. Paul Raymond, the millionaire owner of Raymond's Revue Bar and half Soho, was working in the funfair, earning, he tells me, eight pounds a week and all he could fiddle. Mrs Kingsman, a little old lady in a black dress, not only owned the pier but everything on it. There was a penny admission charge and Ma Kingsman loved to sit in her office over the turnstiles and watch them revolve. I told this to Paul Holt, then showbusiness editor of the *Daily Express*. The next day he headlined his column 'There is Gold on Grandma's Pier'. Unfortunately Grandma was not amused.

Thinking that the time was ripe for a pierrot show in traditional costume. Mr Felix De Wolfe and Mr Richard Stone proudly presented The Pom Poms at the Dolphin Theatre, Brighton. The star and producer was Cliff Gordon. Cliff had written one hit, a Welsh *Our Town* called *Choir Practice* and had a trio of his own revues on BBC television. I thought he was a genius, but had not cottoned on to his drinking. The rehearsals in London were a continual booze-up and on the opening night our star knew not one word of his own script.

We had assembled a splendid little company, including Doris Hare, then known for her wartime radio show *Shipmates Ashore* long before *On The Buses*, and Kenneth Connor. We represented Ken for a bit and I kept getting him jobs in comedy, but he hated the work and me for getting it. He left and buried himself in the Bristol Old Vic, only to emerge as one of the stalwarts of the 'Carry On' films — a classic example of the fool wanting to play Hamlet. Despite their efforts the Pom-Poms were a disaster. Ian Carmichael hurried over from Clacton on the promise of another £20 to rescue the sinking ship, but it sank!

Whilst the music halls were dying, summer shows were thriving. Terry Scott was recommended to me for the Jolly Roger by Evelyn Norris. Evelyn Norris was married to a wealthy financier and lived in a mansion in the stockbroker belt of Surrey, but was stage-struck. During the war she had organised shows for troops in the area. Now she was to act as Terry's agent, and collect ten per cent of the £10 a week which I paid him. She probably gave the pound a week to her chauffeur. I don't see that I did her any lasting damage when I later took over as Terry's agent. She left her money to found the Evelyn Norris home for old 'pros' in Worthing.

Terry auditioned for Ian Carmichael and me in the drawing room of our house on Primrose Hill. He had two main 'turns', firstly the horrid little boy, in which character he had already done a few radio variety shows, and secondly a quick-change routine. He was funny, and we engaged him. He told us then that he had another burlesque, the 'dagger soliloquy' from *Macbeth*, but had no costume in which to perform it. Before rehearsal for Clacton began, I took Terry to Bert Montague's stores and, for £10 I purchased a Macbeth costume. I then deducted a pound a week from Terry's salary for the ten-week run, so that the costume could be his property in perpetuity.

The year 1950 saw the start of a contract which was to be the backbone of my expanding summer seasons. Basil Brown, my colonel from 21 Army Group, had become the Director of Entertainments for Butlins holiday camps. He had decided that each camp was to have a resident revue. He chose three people to produce these shows, Chesney Allen (now retired from Flanagan and Allen and acting as agent for the Crazy Gang), Johnnie Riscoe and myself, his old, troublesome staff captain! We started our association with disaster. Basil and I visited the Artillery Theatre, Woolwich and booked an ex-army comedian, Billy 'Husky' Maxim, who had a very good, if aggressive, stand-up act. I had been given the show at two camps the first year, Skegness and Pwllhelli. Ian Carmichael had gone to produce the first at Skegness, which featured Harry Segal (Benny Hill's sergeant) and it was a great success. The most important thing about these shows was that they must not last more that one hour. Every minute that ran over cost Billy Butlin thousands of pounds in the bar! Next in importance was the geniality of the comedian in his three appearances. The first, welcoming the campers, the second in a sketch and the third, in his own turn. I was directing Pwllhelli myself. Unfortunately Billy Maxim's aggressive approach, which had been right for the Artillery Theatre, Woolwich, was a disaster with a holiday audience. He alienated the 'happy campers' the moment he said 'Hello'. They sat in silence through his sketch and booed his act. I was standing at the back of the theatre with Billy Butlin.

'He'll have to go, Richard.'

'When?'

'Tonight.'

All of us connected with entertainment were in a special line of chalets,

73

and I lay in bed that night deep in gloom. It was indeed not difficult to be gloomy in a Butlin's chalet, even when things were going well. The camps had only very recently been rescued from their wartime use as army barracks. The chalets had only an iron bedstead, a tin cupboard and a cold tap, and the baths and toilets were several chalet lines away. My only comfort was being next to Ivy Benson and her all-girls band! I was skimming through *The Stage* and found an advertisement, 'Available for Summer Season, Cliff Weir, Family Entertainer, late of "The Queeries" Concert Party'. He might be just the man, so, early the next morning, I phoned him. He was available. Yes, he had been in The Queeries concert party in the war. Yes, he had plenty of material. He was told to meet Ian Carmichael the next morning on Paddington Station. I then phoned Ian and gave him what must have been the most absurd instruction ever from an impresario to his assistant: 'If Cliff Weir looks warm and funny, put him on the first train to Bangor. If he doesn't, send him home!'

I went to Bangor myself to meet Cliff Weir in a Butlins shooting brake. He had certainly plenty of costumes. We loaded six skips into the van. He was quite an old man and I was therefore not surprised to learn that the Queeries concert party in which he had featured was not in my war, but in 1914! However, he looked warm. He was 'on' that night. He seemed quite merry and welcomed the campers in a jolly fashion. His sketch was so-so. It was when he came on to do his act in a striped blazer and straw hat and sang a song which contained the phrase 'The poached egg sat down on the toast and jolly old summer is here' that Billy Butlin exploded again.

'He'll have to go, Richard.'

'When?'

'Tonight.'

Ultimately, at great expense, I got hold of that lovely comedian Freddie Frinton, with his famous sketch 'Dinner for One'. At the time Freddie was disgruntled for, to use the pro's excuse, 'owing to unforeseen circumstances he surprisingly found himself vacant'. He thought his agent was booking him into the Opera House, Blackpool, and he landed up at Butlins Pwllhelli.

Incidentally, 'Dinner for One' is still shown every New Year's Eve on network TV throughout Germany. To our amazement, it was shown to us recently after the captain's dinner on a German freighter and the officers fell about, presumably for the umpteenth time.

Billy Butlin was good fun in those days. I remember there was a flood one year at Skegness which went right through the chalets. I was commiserating with Bill.

'Oh it's not too bad, Richard. I've saved all the mattresses, they were all stained with water. I've put new mattresses in at Skegness and taken the stained ones up to Filey. They won't look under the sheets at Filey.'

His only serious rival in the holiday camp world was Pontin. A share-holder at the annual general meeting asked Billy what he knew of Pontin.

'Fred Pontin, I taught him all he knows. Not all I know, mind you, just all he knows'

I was getting a bit cocky now, and although only 30 years old, I thought I was Charles B. Cochran. I put out a brochure which makes amusing reading now, both for its sheer audacity and the cast list of my staff!

THIS BROCHURE is sent to you in an endeavour to interest you in our summer shows for future seasons. We hope that it may whet your appetite sufficiently for you to make even an uncomfortable journey to see whichever show is nearest to you.

We employ young artistes, and a team of young producers and script writers under the personal supervision of Richard Stone. Each show is, therefore, planned and directed by a producer and the fourth and fifth programmes are presented with the same polish and the same detailed rehearsal as No. 1.

THE PRODUCTION TEAM

RICHARD STONE . . . . *in charge of Production*

Before the war was on the other side of the footlights as a straight actor and in Concert Party. After 4 years in the Gunners, transferred to Army Entertainments and was finally responsible as Lt.-Colonel in charge of production at the War Office for C.S.E. shows throughout the world. The firm of Felix de Wolfe and Richard Stone exclusively represents some of the leading artistes in all branches of the entertainment world.

IAN CARMICHAEL . . . . *Producer*

This brilliant young artiste, who was recently playing the light comedy lead in "Wild Violets" at the Stoll Theatre, London, is rapidly making a name for himself as a producer. Currently appearing in two television series, "Don't Look Now" and "Regency Room," he has now been asked to produce for television.

DAVID CROFT . . . . *Assistant Producer and Script Writer*

Another up-and-coming all-rounder, this younger son of Musical Comedy Star Anne Croft, brings a great knowledge of every branch of the theatre to our shows. With his brother, Peter, currently starring in Sir Charles Cochran's "Bless the Bride," he recently wrote special comedy scenes for Leo Franklyn in "Belinda Fair."

EX LT.-COL. (Reduced to Theatrical Agency)
and ACTRESS WIFE (Retired on Income
from repeat fees) are still living, not only
together, but at 7 ST. GEORGE'S TERRACE,
N.W.1. (The Eaton Square of CHALK FARM).
They Offer these premises on a short lease to their
friends for the NIGHT OF DEC. 31st FROM
ABOUT 10 P.M. for eating, drinking and WEL-
COMING IN THE NEW YEAR.

R.S.V.P.

With apologies to E. H. Brooks & Son.

Our second son, Tim, was born on Christmas Day 1948, which effectively prevented Sara from playing pantomime. It also meant moving from our cottage in Manchester Street. We bought a six-storeyed terraced house overlooking Primrose Hill, and lived there until 1971. Number 7 St George's Terrace had a large living room on the first floor which ran the length of the house, and had a beautiful, decorated ceiling. We threw great New Year's Eve parties in that room when show business friends trooped in and out from 10 o'clock to dawn. In a little room upstairs we installed a fortune teller. She told a pianist friend 'You walk a lot in your job, my dear.'

'If you call walking to the piano a lot, I suppose I do.'

Ian Wallace was told to give up show business. He advised me to get rid of her if I wanted to keep my clients.

There was a little strip of communal garden in front of the 11 houses in St George's Terrace. We put in a concrete slab on our frontage, and here our children slept in their old-fashioned perambulators in all weather. With Sara working we had to have a nanny. Ours was a character. The children had to be in bed by 6.45 so that she could listen to *The Archers*. And if I came home from the office before seven, I waited before I dared ask after my children.

Our daughter Diana was born in November 1950, just in time for Sara to fulfil another pantomime engagement as Cinderella in Sheffield. Then, in 1951, she landed the leading girl's role opposite George Formby in *Zip Goes a Million*. Beryl Formby, George's wife, was still a monster and totally dominated George. She collected his earnings, and doled him out pocket money. One of the few pleasures she allowed him was to wash his Rolls-Royce on Sunday mornings. He had an eye for the girls, and made a bee-line for Sara. So Beryl stood in the wings for every single performance for a year to monitor their stage romance. On odd nights she would even carry out a spot check by secreting herself behind the sofa on stage!

Sara's next West End show immediately followed *Zip*. In fact, the impresario Lord Anthony Vivian arrived unannounced in her dressing room at the Palace Theatre and asked her if she would star (top billing for the first time in London) in a revival of Herbert and Eleanor Farjeon's *The*

Two Bouquets. It was in this show that she started a friendship that was to last a lifetime. The other leading lady was Sonia Williams (wife of actor Nigel Stock) playing her cousin. They opened at the St Martin's Theatre a few weeks before *The Mousetrap* next door at The Ambassador. Although they didn't run as long they achieved a very respectable nine months.

Sonia, who just before I retired became my secretary and nurse-maid (she hid my cigars!), was an invaluable help in the early stages of this epic, interpreting and typing my almost illegible scrawls.

In 1951 Terry Scott was going to Butlins Skegness and we decided to back him with a 'second' comedian. A young milkman from Leicester who had been working part-time in the clubs applied for the job. He auditioned in the same drawing room as Terry Scott exactly one year later. He played the banjo, sang George Formby songs and was not particularly original, but he had an engaging personality. We liked him, but not his name, Billy Williams. So he changed it to Bill Maynard. Terry was now on £13 a week and Bill was starting at £10. However, they augmented their meagre salaries by 10s a week each – appropriating the pound I had allocated for laundry and doing the company's washing between them.

We had some exciting holidays in the early 1950s. We went with Gordon Wixley, a fellow officer from 5RHA, to Italy, and tried, unsuccessfully, to find our billets in Salerno. We then stayed for a week in Positano. Before leaving England, I had casually asked Benny Hill to join us. Unfortunately the jelly-fish in Positano nearly drove us mad and we decamped to Taormina in Sicily, whereupon Benny turned up in Positano to find us flown. Another year we took our two small boys by car all through the Pyrenees. Running out of petrol high in the mountains, we free-wheeled downhill and found ourselves in Cadaques, where we stayed two weeks. Barry infuriated Salvador Dali who lived nearby, by disturbing his swans!

Throughout my career I have been blessed with a special relationship involving an ever-changing panorama of impresarios and film producers. 'Men may come and men may go, but I'll be the vicar of Bray, sir.' It must have been in 1949 that I struck up a friendship with Bertram Montague. Bert would then have been in his fifties, an enthusiastic and loveable little Jewish gentleman. He was the outsider in the pantomime world. Emile and Prince Littler and Tom Arnold had the very best dates. Bert had the next best. He loved pantomime with a passion amounting almost to madness. He bought the Princes (now the Shaftesbury) Theatre for the sole purpose of showing London that a Bertram Montague pantomime was better that anything Emile Littler could produce at the Coliseum, or Val Parnell at the Palladium. The Princes was a white elephant and Bert had difficulty in booking shows for the rest of the year. Luckily in 1949 he was the landlord to a smash hit, *His Excellency*, starring Eric Portman. But

Bert had bought the Princes for his pantomimes and so he threw out his one money-making hit in time for Christmas!

I booked a lot of artistes into *Dick Whittington* that year, including Sara as Alice Fitzwarren and my old school chum Ian Wallace as the Emperor. On the opening night, in Morocco, after Dick Whittington's cat had rid the palace of rats, the Emperor wished to show his gratitude to Dick and announced a special entertainment. Twelve Arab acrobats, booked at enormous expense as a climax to the pantomime, should have appeared. Regrettably, they were still practising jumping onto each other's shoulders deep in the bowels of the theatre, and missed their entrance. The Highgate Hill Cloth was lowered and Dick Whittington, now back in triumph in dear old London, entered to wind up the evening. Bert was in the stage box taking photographs. The thought of £500 a week's worth of Arabs being totally cut was too much to bear. He ran through the pass door like a dose of salts and, much to the astonishment of Dick Whittington, pushed on his Arabs to perform on Highgate Hill! On another night when Nelson, incongruously introduced to wind up the first half of the pantomime, was delivering a patriotic monologue, disaster struck again. The flat which represented the bridge of his ship fell down, revealing him as Nelson only from the waist up. Below he was the hind legs of the pantomime horse!

In his determination to become the king of pantomime, Bert sought to create a unique monopoly. There were only so many speciality artistes playing the animals in pantomime; the cat in *Dick Whittington*, the goose in *Mother Goose* etc. These artistes had their own skins and basically only worked at Christmas. So, Bert signed up the best at annual salaries of approximately £2,000 for life. This worked out well when Bert had several shows which ran for ten weeks or more, so that he was paying £200 a week or less for a very specialised service. But sadly later on, Bert's pantomime world grew smaller and smaller and he was forced ultimately to present shows in some pretty ghastly dumps for four weeks or less, where his cat was costing £500 a week, probably more than his star!

The 1950s were the last great days of the music hall and variety. I spent a lot of evenings chasing around London in my pre-war Morris 8, between Camberwell, Lewisham, Hackney, Chiswick and Shepherds Bush. Variety bills followed a pattern. The first turn was usually a cheap dance act consisting of a boy and girl or two girls. Next on, in the dreaded number two spot, was the unknown comedian. Then came another, more expensive 'spec', acrobats, jugglers, a ventriloquist, Kardomah, 'who filled the stage with flags', or Marquis, a randy chimpanzee who had to be kept away from the girls. The 'second top', maybe a singer, closed the first half and the star closed the second half.

The Metropolitan, Edgware Road, was typical of its kind and was a Mecca for the variety agents. There was a bar at the back of the stalls where we all gathered and could view the proceedings through the glass panels. Many of the variety agents were also booking agents for one or more theatres, and a lot of business was done in the bar. When his number came up in the illuminated box at the side of the stage I would hustle the agent Bill Henschel into the back of the stalls, so that Terry Scott could get a week at the Middlesbrough Empire.

There were over 50 variety theatres in and around London alone so that a cockney comedian, one Ernie Lotinga, who had his own show, never had to leave town.

In addition to the number one and number two dates, there were the dreaded 'number threes', fleapits where the likes of Archie Rice from John Osborne's *The Entertainer* topped the bill. Before she hit the top, Alma Cogan, playing a split week on the number three circuit in Wales, arrived on the Thursday morning in Pontypridd to complete the second half of the week. The theatre was deserted except for an old lady cleaning the stalls. Alma asked what time is the band call. The old lady put down her mop and bucket and, rubbing her hands on her apron, walked to the piano and said, 'Any time you like, dear!'

Hutch, the celebrated and sophisticated black entertainer at the piano, is starring on a provincial tour and has engaged his own supporting company. As he is not appearing until the second half he comes in late after the curtain has gone up, passes on his way out the young comedian he has engaged to open the show. Hutch asks him what the audience is like, to which the young man tactlessly replies, 'Hardly worth blacking up for!'

The date that all the acts aspired to was the Finsbury Park Empire, for this was on the number one Moss Empire circuit and could lead to a date at the London Palladium. The booker for Moss Empires was the formidable Cissie Williams. Cissie would be in every first house Monday with her assistant, one Ted Gollop, who would be sent round before the second house with Cissie's criticism of the acts. The story goes that Ted Gollop retires and Cissie puts an advertisement in *The Stage* for a new assistant. Applicants are to parade on Monday at the back of the stalls at the Finsbury Park Empire. Cissie lines them up, and issues the command, 'First one through the pass door gets the job!'

The next best thing to the Finsbury Park Empire was a booking on the syndicate halls, Chelsea, Brixton and the Metropolitan, Edgware Road. These three dates were booked by another influential lady, Miss Leddington. It was known that Miss Leddington could be more easily influenced than Cissie Williams. The comic, Johnnie Riscoe, was walking down the Kings Road one Saturday morning, following Miss Leddington. In his hand was a string bag full of groceries. A fellow comic, passing by, asks Johnny what he has got in the shopping bag and Johnny replies, 'I've got the Met, June twentieth, Chelsea June twenty-seventh and Brixton July fourth!'

There was once another syndicate hall, Walthamstow Palace. The managing director was asked how he was doing at Walthamstow. 'I've closed it,' he replied. 'And if that's a success, I shall close the others.'

In fact I helped to close the other syndicate halls in 1957. In desperation, when the music halls were fast folding, Cecil Bernstein of Granada, whose firm had bought the theatres, asked if I could devise some entertainment to keep the doors open. We put on a sort of summer show in London starring Terry Scott and Hugh Lloyd called *The London Revue*. It was pretty ghastly and did not prevent the demolition of Brixton and the Met and the conversion of the Chelsea Palace into a Granada TV studio.

My very happiest memory of a summer show was Lyme Regis 1952. Chesney Allen was producing quite a sizeable show in Weymouth, and for some reason this had lumbered him with the obligation to present a much smaller show at Lyme. He was only too happy to sublet the date to me. Ches had already engaged Harold Berens ('Wot a Geezer') and there was not much money left for the rest of the cast. Hugh Lloyd was in the Middle East for Combined Services Entertainment with Harry Secombe. He was drinking champagne in the officers mess when he received my telegram: 'Can offer you ten week season in Lyme Regis, second comic and manage company – £11 a week'.

He finished his glass of champagne and wired back his acceptance. The soprano was Peggy Thompson, Sara's Prince Charming from Sheffield. Peggy had the advantage of a good wardrobe and so was able to appear in front of our piece of decorated trellis dressed as a principal boy in a scene called 'Pages from Pantomime'. The baritone was William Dickie, who had sung Don José in *Carmen* at Covent Garden and was now working part-time for De Wolfe and Stone. Bill finally gave up singing and became my right-hand man and dear friend until he so sadly died, much too young, in 1982. On and off the stage he had a wonderful and loud voice. A friend asked me once if Bill had got a telephone yet, or did he still communicate direct!

David Croft produced the show at Lyme Regis, on his honeymoon. David, his wife Ann and I arrived in the beautiful but tiny resort of Lyme Regis and went straight to find our theatre. It was not much more than a grand shed clinging to the side of the rocks. We had sent down posters for the show but they were still in the town hall beside the theatre. The only posters on display were for the amateur production of *Aladdin* the previous Christmas! Ann Croft spent her honeymoon with me, sticking up posters. To make up for the lack of advance publicity, we engaged the town crier. For 3s 6d he called the short cry up and down the front. The long cry round the town cost 5 shillings.

'Oyez, oyez, tonight in the Marine Theatre *Lymelight Rendezvous* starring Harold Berens, Hugh Lloyd and Anthea Askey.' So short of cash were we that many nights we had to dip into the meagre box office takings to pay him.

Harold Berens and Hugh Lloyd were both available for Christmas, and wanted to be together for pantomime. Bert Montague was in need of robbers for *Babes in the Wood*. I drove him in my Morris 8 all the way to Lyme Regis.

In the afternoon Harold, Bert, Hugh and I went out mackerel fishing. Bert was in his best business suit with his gold watch and chain and trilby hat. We chugged about all the afternoon and caught nothing. At about 5.30 the mackerel started to bite, and Bert was really enjoying himself. I had to make a snap decision whether to go on fishing or take the stars back for their first performance. There were never more than a handful of people in at 6.30 and I decided they could come back tomorrow. So we went on catching mackerel, and Harold and Hugh got their pantomime!

Terry and Bill came together again in 1955 for the television series *Great Scott, it's Maynard*, which was partly variety but with a sketch content. It was a forerunner of today's situation comedy. After two series, it began to flounder as it became less clear who was the star. At first Bill accepted the seniority of Terry, and was happy to 'feed' him. As Bill's reputation increased rather rapidly, the situation became fraught. They each demanded their own series. Ironically, though *Great Scott, it's Maynard* had been an unqualified success, their solo series, called *Mostly Maynard* and *Scott Free* were unqualified disasters. Terry and Bill remained good clients always.

It is sad that *Terry and June* came to personify wall-to-wall domestic comedy. It was so good for many many series. I was fishing on the Spey some years ago, too involved to read newspapers. Consequently, I missed the headline about the sex life of the 'Bournemouth Bonker', in *The News of the World*. Apparently Terry had been having it off with the bank manager's daughter. I forget how and why it all came out, but I do remember that he accused his darling wife of being useless in bed and a lesbian, despite her having given him four lovely daughters. Terry was an appalling big mouth. Let loose with a journalist or, even worse, on a live television interview, he would pontificate and talk the most abject nonsense whilst firmly believing he was uttering pearls of wisdom. He talked an equal amount of rubbish to his employers, telling them how to do their business, and telling his fellow actors how to act. However, I loved him. Of all my clients, I think he had the greatest respect for my advice. He had serious brain surgery at one time, and we all wondered if he would ever work again. But he was brave, if foolish. He took on a short summer season at Weymouth. I went to the opening night, and in the car park, after the performance, he fell on my shoulder and said that, without me, he would not have wished to carry on in show business. That, to an agent, is worth 'a guinea a box'.

It was in 1960 that I was asked to go to the Collins, Islington, a number two date in North London. It had a famous bar which ran down the side of the stalls, where the audience mingled with the artistes. Once a rodeo act brought their horse into the bar. The manager objected. The cowboy said his horse was an artiste and should be allowed in the bar. 'Yes,' said the manager, 'but not in his make-up.'

My visit was to see an act, Al and Dave Page, which featured a young Irishman who had just finished a season as a Butlins Redcoat. I liked him, and so began a lifelong association with Dave Allen. Dave is a remarkable character. He was probably the first comedian to leave behind his jokes and start commenting on life. He is the least 'theatrical' person I have ever met. His work is arranged to take him to places in the world he wants to see. When he has completed the work he often goes walkabout, some-times for nearly a year. When not travelling he is at home painting. And, unlike most pros, he never talks about himself. He once played Captain Hook in *Peter Pan* with his friend Maggie Smith at the Coliseum. The sea-son opened with a matinee and I sat in front with my son Barry, on a visit from Toronto. Everything went wrong at the matinee: the sound was hope-lessly distorted and a drunken lady in the stalls kept up a barrage of shouted advice to the actors. Any other actor visited by his agent after such a performance would have been in hysterics, not Dave Allen. He welcomed us, thanked us for coming, and proceeded to enquire deeply into how Barry was faring in Canada! Early in his career I booked Dave to be second comic in one of Hedley Claxton's Gaytime companies, in a tent on Plymouth Hoe! The star was George Lacey, who whilst being the high-est paid and best pantomime dame in the country, had difficulty in finding employment for the rest of the year. Dave bought himself a new alpaca suit with a lovely sheen. Hedley, who had a lisping falsetto voice which could have fooled you that he was gay, caught Dave ironing his suit. 'Don't, don't!' he screamed. 'You'll make it all shiny!'

Dave showed too much promise at Plymouth. There were six changes of programme, produced by George Lacey. In programme number one, Dave made six appearances. By programme number six, he was making one!

My next special relationship was with Bernard Delfont. It was a strange friendship. We were opposites. Bernie, a Russian émigré with an East End upbringing, ambitious, with no outside interests and determined to fight his way to the top. Me, the son of a reasonably wealthy stockbroker, with a public school education, the security of a little money and a lot of outside interests. I think Bernie was impressed by my background, although his belief in the integrity of the English public school boy was shaken when his old Etonian accountant disappeared with the petty cash! At this time, Bernie was temporarily (not for the first time or last time) hard up. I picked him up most mornings from his flat, on the other side of Primrose Hill, and drove him to his office. His brothers, Lew and Leslie Grade, who controlled as agents most of the variety stars of the day, had little love to spare for this Richard Stone who was building a useful stable of new star comedians and now was getting much too friendly with brother Bernie. Gracie Fields had been booked by Bernie to star in a variety bill at the Prince of Wales. I was quick off the mark and sold him, probably on the way to work in my car, two of my comics to support Gracie. Jon Pertwee, already a name from radio, was in the cherished spot closing the first half, Terry Scott, as then relatively unknown, in the dreaded second spot.

Terry was allotted eight minutes. The week before, he was involved in a car crash and came straight, and in a slightly dazed condition, from Watford hospital to the theatre. Instead of eight minutes, he gave the audience the benefit of his three routines, the Little Boy, the Quick Change, and the Shakespeare, a total of 28 minutes!! The show overran so badly that Gracie Fields had to cut out two songs. Val Parnell, whose company owned the Prince of Wales theatre, was outraged. He was letting off steam to Bernie between houses and I was hovering.

'Get that man out of my theatre, I won't have him in the second house!'

I grabbed Bernie's arm. 'I promise, Bernie, that if you can persuade Val, I'll guarantee Terry only does eight minutes.'

Val calmed down and I went round to Terry's dressing room and removed two of his costumes. The next morning, I had cause to phone Bernie, and by some strange chance his switchboard plugged me through while he was talking to brother Lew. On the crossed line I heard Lew utter the immortal words, 'Terry Scott doing twenty-eight minutes on the Gracie Fields bill. That Richard Stone has got you fucking mesmerised!'

There is a Grade story I love concerning a fellow agent. Peter Prichard as a young lad was paid £5 a week by Lew and Leslie and wanted a rise. One Saturday morning he persuaded Leslie to take him in to see Lew, the senior partner. He told Lew that he wanted a rise and Lew asked him how much.

'Well, the cigars I fetch for you each morning cost ten pounds. What about ten pounds?'

'Boy, when you give me as much satisfaction as those cigars I'll pay you ten pounds!'

Everyone loves Harry Secombe. His warmth on stage is only a reflection of the man himself. I looked after him for six months, doing a 'locum' for his own agent who was ill. I booked him into Cyril Fletcher's *Magpies* at Torquay, and was shattered to receive several letters from the Torquay council complaining of this 'dirty comedian', until it transpired that the offence was littering the stage with soap during his shaving act.

In those early years I built up a stable of maybe 20 comedians and comedy actors. Half of them became stars, and what of the other half? I believed as much in them, but sadly they never quite came to the very top of the pile. Maybe they were as funny as their more successful contemporaries, but just lacked that great gift of being an 'original'. There is a lovely man, Felix Bowness, who makes a few appearances in situation comedies, but his main claim to fame is as the best 'warm-up' man in the business. Most nights, sometimes in two studios at once, Felix can be found keeping the audience chuckling whilst the scenery is being moved and the actors are changing their costumes. If he spotted me around, his gags included, 'My agent is in front tonight. Thirty years ago he promised me I'd be a star and look at me now, just a little twinkle.'

The British film industry after the war produced a spate of escapist comedy films. First and foremost in the field were Michael Balcon's Ealing comedies. It was therefore to Sir Michael that I offered my first and biggest star, Benny Hill. Sir Michael gave us his top scriptwriter, T.E.B. Clarke, and the very clever director Basil Dearden. It should have been another *Passport to Pimlico* or *Kind Hearts and Coronets*. Sadly, all these great talents did not produce a winner and any one of them, if asked, would have replied in answer to the film's title *Who Dunnit?* 'Not me.'

Peter Rogers and Gerald Thomas were making the Carry On films. Jackie Piper was a pretty young client whom Peter Rogers wanted under contract. I wrote a short letter to Peter stating that Jackie Piper would make six films for him at various increasing fees, the dates to be mutually agreed, as was the billing. Peter wrote back 'Dear Richard, Jackie Piper. I agree. Love Peter.' This arrangement worked perfectly for 6 years. Today there would be lawyers on both sides arguing about a 20-page contract for months on end!

There were the St Trinians films, and the Rank Organisation's *Doctor in the House* series, and lesser imitations with titles like *Dentist on the Job*. Shirley Eaton was in so much demand that at one time she was working on four films at once! These films cost between £100,000 and £150,000 and made a profit on their first release in the UK. Today it is impossible to make a film solely for the UK cinema market. However, with the help of backing from TV and the recent success of films like *Four Weddings and a Funeral, Bean* and *The Full Monty* in the States, things are looking up.

I had a special relationship in the film world, with the Boulting brothers. My introduction to them was bizarre. Ian Carmichael was starring in 'The Globe Revue' in the West End and the Boulting brothers were looking for a newcomer to play the lead in *Private's Progress*. One of their wives had seen Ian and had laughed at him 'undressing on the beach'. She couldn't

Me in sailor suit

Me and my brother

My father

My grandfather and father
with brother Michael and me

Scholars Court, Charterhouse, probably 1936. I am 5th from the right

Photo courtesy of Sport & General Press Agency Limited

Me on the far left in *French Without Tears*, Colchester Rep 1939

My 'Repro' when an actor, sent out with my C.V.

Sara Gregory

Sara and I outside Ruby House, Saltburn 1939

Me playing an old man
in the Regency Players
at Huddersfield in 1939

My return visit to Ruby House in 1999

Saltburn Pier

Photo courtesy Syndication International Ltd

2nd Lt. Stone
Photo courtesy Basil Shackleton

On the outbreak of war Felix De Wolfe organised some troop shows for Air Force bases. I am
the fairy queen
Photo courtesy The Croydon Advertiser

Me and Sara on our wedding day

The Circus Belli in Hamburg with Hagenbachs big top

Ian Carmichael and me in our 30 Corps production of *Springtime for Henry* with two ENSA girls

Sara in *Zip Goes a Million* with George Formby   Photo courtesy Houston Mogen

Sara in her dressing room at the St James Theatre playing Cinderella. The photo is me, the baby is our first child - Barry

The family home in Gloucestershire - The Hermitage

Me and the children
- I think at Frinton

Sara, me and our
three children in the
drawing room of
7 St Georges Terrace

Photo courtesy Eric Coop

'A conference of comics' - clockwise from left: Dave Allen, Nicholas Parsons, Norman Vaughan, Lance Percival, Brian Rix, Benny Hill, Richard Stone, Janet Gardiner (my secretary who also doubled as Ian Lavender's mum in *Dad's Army*) Fred Emney, Cardew Robinson, Jon Pertwee, Terry Scott, Hugh Lloyd, Eric Barker. This photo appeared in the *Daily Express* in 1965 with the headline 'The £250,000 laugh-spinners'. £250,000 was the joint annual income of everyone around that table

Photo courtesy London Express

Sara and I discussing our shows produced for Butlins with Billy Butlin
Photo courtesy Matthews News and Photo Agency

Richard Stone the fisherman

From left to right: Benny Hill, Dennis Kirkland (Benny's director), Me and Philip Jones

Toasting Danny La Rue at the opening of our Winter Gardens Margate show

Me at the races to see our horse 'Parisien Star' (co-owned with Paul Elliot) with two of my grandchildren - Ben and Miranda 1999

even remember his name, so Roy rang the management, who referred them to me. So began Ian's film career, which was shortly to make him Britain's number one box office attraction.

When the Boultings had a script ready for casting they would send it to all the agents, but only I and one other were subsequently summoned to give our casting suggestions in person. It was a frightening experience, being ushered into Roy and John's office. I could never tell which was which, only that I was outnumbered! They sat there like two caustic head-masters and delighted in treating me as one of their most insignificant pupils. I remembered I had persuaded them to use Eric Barker in *Brothers in Law*, for which Eric had received an *Evening Standard* award as the best newcomer that year in films. I was therefore fairly confident in recommending him for the part of a police sergeant in their next film.

'Don't be ridiculous, Richard,' snapped one of them. 'He's a midget.'

I explained, with some trepidation, that Eric was large enough to be playing a policeman in a current TV series.

'Very small screen,' snapped the other.

Eric Barker was a talented man. After his wartime success in *Merry-go-round*, he had his own series of revues on television in the 1950s. His satirical humour was way ahead of its time. Sadly he had a severe stroke whilst still in his prime. When he died a few years ago, he was forgotten. Sara and I were the only people from show business at his funeral.

I had a good relationship with a dynamic little American film producer, Hal Chester. Hal had been, as a boy, a member of Hal Roach's 'Our Gang' in the Hollywood comedies. We used to play golf on Saturdays at Highgate. Hal was one of a small group of wheeler-dealers whose heyday was in the 1950s. If Hal seemed to have the necessary ingredients, he could get a hundred per cent finance from a major company. For example, he 'expressed an interest' in the film rights of *School for Scoundrels*. He told Ian Carmichael that he'd already got the rights and the services of Terry Thomas. He told Terry Thomas he'd already got the rights and Ian Carmichael. He told Warner Bros he'd already got all three! Having, in one weekend, obtained these agreements, he confirmed the deals on Monday, and Warner Bros coughed up all the money.

Bernie Delfont, guided by his clever lieutenant Billy Marsh, was sign-ing up all the up-and-coming young comics to long-term theatre contracts, including Bill Maynard, who had by now earned a considerable reputation as a stand-up comic, the first to appear casually dressed in a sweater. Bernie asked me if I would like to produce a summer show in Weymouth for him, to star Bill. I think Bernie was financially stretched at the time and welcomed the fact that I would be providing the costumes and scenery! I remember having to buy a blue sweater for my star to appear in the finale. All the other men were in dinner jackets but it was against Bill's image to be so formal. The first sweater my wardrobe department produced was too small and I nobbled it. It is still my favourite old fishing sweater and lives on my boat in the Isle of Wight!

We made a handsome profit on the show of which I was due half, but it took over a year to get it, for the Delfont office had been in receipt of the takings. Bernie owed a lot of folk a lot of money at that time. Every Friday I would send Bill Roberton round to Jermyn Street, where he would join a queue of creditors.

Greg Smith, then starting his career as the office boy, would be sent out to assess the weight of the enemy and they would each be fobbed off with a few hundred pounds and an invitation to come back next Friday.

We produced the show again the next year at Weymouth, starring Charlie Drake. Amongst the hopeful girl singers we auditioned was an 18-year-old Barbara Windsor. Apparently I thought she was good but turned her down on the grounds that she was too small and too like Charlie Drake. Bill Roberton found her outside the rehearsal room in tears. She thought she was a sex symbol even then and 'E bleeding well tells me I look like Charlie Drake!'

The third year I introduced Scarborough to the partnership, and as it was my date and Benny Hill was the star, I foolishly billed the show as 'Richard Stone and Bernard Delfont present', unwisely putting my name first. Dear Bernie, in his autobiography *East End, West End*, attributed our parting of the ways to finding my name on his scenery – untrue, as always in our business, it was the billing!

The Benny Hill show destined for Scarborough had a rough ride. We booked a very young musical director. Regrettably, his experience as a fixer of musicians was limited. When we opened for a try-out week at Stockton-on-Tees all hell broke loose. The orchestra were totally incapable of playing any of the music. I have a vivid memory of an elderly lady banging away on a kettle drum. I phoned Bernie in a panic and he sent up the musical director from the Prince of Wales to sort it out. Harold Collins attended the dress rehearsal with a representative of the Musicians Union from Newcastle. Even the MU could not justify the appalling noise that was being perpetrated and, with their full consent, the entire orchestra were sacked and we finally opened with a brand-new set of real musicians. But our troubles were not quite over. The speciality in the show was a husband-and-wife act who performed comedy balancing on a high wire stretched across the stage. They were very good at Stockton, but when they put up their apparatus on the small stage at the Floral Hall, Scarborough, their wire was up in the flies and they were quite invisible to the audience! It was not their fault and I had to pay them off with their entire salary for the season.

The start of commercial television in 1955 was good for De Wolfe and

Stone. Lew and Leslie Grade went into television with a vengeance and by introducing a large investment from Val Parnell of Moss Empires, Lew found himself Deputy Managing Director right away. So harassed were they at the start that they even welcomed a weekly excerpt from London musical shows booked by *me* into *Sunday Night at the Palladium*! There was a great demand for speciality acts and Topo Gigio, a mouse puppet, was given many return engagements. One Saturday, Alec Fine, the booker in the Grade office, rushed in to Lew and told him with great glee that he had managed to get Tito Gobbi for tomorrow's show.

'Oh Lord,' Lew moaned. 'Not that bloody mouse again.'

The other London-based company, Rediffusion, was run from the bridge by a certain Commander Brownrigg and a staff with much experience of life at sea but with little knowledge of show business. Felix De Wolfe had some sort of previous connection with Brownrigg, and this gave De Wolfe and Stone a head start. We sent for interview every struggling writer and actor we represented who fancied the security of a staff job in television, and they all got taken on, including David Croft as some sort of script editor. When my old friends George and Alfred Black were awarded the contract to start Tyne Tees Television, David moved there as a trainee director. Later he moved to the BBC, where, with *Dad's Army*, it all began to happen for him.

In the 1950s, I had my one and almost only contact with the pop world. Norrie Paramor, at that time a recording manager for EMI, had spotted a young vocalist with Eric Winston's band and gave him a recording contract.

Thinking he now needed an agent, Norrie recommended me. So I came to represent Michael Holiday. At the beginning it was a happy association. Michael was a shy, complex but very loveable guy. He was not easy to understand. He had a string of hit records and at one time three numbers in the Top Ten and his own TV series. He was playing Finsbury Park Empire when it all began to go wrong. On the bill with him was Hal Monty. Monty had done everything in show business, even at one time partnering Bernard Delfont in a dance act, The Delfont Boys. He had some success during the war as a comic on radio, but times were hard and he now needed another string to his bow. He persuaded Michael that he needed a personal manager. From then on Monty and I pulled in opposite directions. I was concerned with Michael's future, Hal was concerned with making a quick buck. Michael was not one to be put under pressure and Monty kept overbooking him behind my back. Finally Monty persuaded Michael that he didn't need me and took over all his business. Shortly afterwards, Michael committed suicide.

In 1959 I made my first trip to New York and stayed for the first time in the famed Algonquin. I couldn't have been in better company, for I went with Ronnie Waldman, then head of BBC Television Light Entertainment.

But even the BBC in those early days meant nothing in America. I kept knocking on doors that wouldn't open. It's all changed now and America recognises the superiority of British television and the wealth of British talent.

Sara had given up her career to concentrate on looking after the children. The boys were at boarding school. We sent them both to my old schools, Aldro and Charterhouse. It was when Barry was so upset that Sara had missed seeing him win the hundred yards whilst she was performing a matinee of *Zip Goes a Million* that she decided to quit.

If I have a regret about those years after the war it is that I alas was too busy to spend enough time with my children. After serving six years in the army, building a new career seemed all-important. I was working 16 hours a day at my two jobs as agent and impresario. Often I would leave the office in the late afternoon, drive or take the train, to a seaside resort and supervise a dress rehearsal until the early hours. Then drive or take a sleeper home, to be back in the office for the morning.

The 1950s ended for me on a sad note. My beloved father died on Christmas Eve 1959. He had forgiven me for going on the stage. He had been proud of my exploits in the desert and had even, after the war, wanted to buy me a theatre. He had given me the capital to start the agency and lent me the money to buy our home. But, most of all, he had shown me, by his example, standards of behaviour towards my fellow human beings, which I am still striving to maintain today.

9

The tide turns at Weymouth, Lance Percival,
Danny la Rue – and Benny Hill leaves the BBC

The 1960s didn't start all that well. We went skiing and I twisted my foot badly. In those days safety bindings were a luxury which I chose to forgo. My right ski went under a ridge of ice and I fell, pulling every ligament possible. No amount of operations, massage or physiotherapy ever put it right, and, 40 years later, it still aches like hell after 18 holes of golf!

In 1960 we first went to Seaview in the Isle of Wight, went on going, and now live there. Seaview lies between Ryde and Bembridge, looking directly back to Portsmouth across the Solent. There are two small hotels and no boarding houses, and consequently few 'grockles', the name by which conventional holidaymakers are dismissed by the locals. The same families, with holiday homes, come to Seaview for generation after generation. So it is the grandchildren of our original friends who are now sailing and attending the dinghy dances in our small yacht club.

For the first years we rented a house for the whole of August. Linen and cutlery were sent down, luggage in advance. Then we all, including the dog, piled into our new Ford Consul, crossed the Solent and the clock was turned back 60 years to the Victorian Age. We had a tent on the beach and a Seaview dinghy, in which I and the children learnt to sail. It took quite a time to be accepted by the 'yachties', as the sailing fraternity are known, and to interpret their greeting, 'How long are you darn fah?'

It took much longer to be accepted by the village. It was in fact 35 years after we arrived that Gerald Caws, the proprietor of the local shoe shop ('The Best Sand Shoes in Town'), father of the local builder, President of the Garden Society and head of a Seaview family going back many generations, said to my wife, 'Please call me Gerald.'

It was also in 1960 that I tamed my ambition. I was piqued at being thrown out by Bernard Delfont and was determined to play David to his Goliath. We had started our partnership at the Alexandra Gardens, Weymouth, an old-fashioned wooden summer season theatre. The corporation had begun work in the autumn of 1959 for an opening in 1960 of a brand new Pavilion Theatre. Bernie was given first refusal of the date but decided to stick with the Alexandra Gardens. Right, I thought, I'll show him. We decided on an August Bank Holiday opening. I persuaded Cyril Stapleton to bring the entire BBC Show Band as an on-stage attraction. There were 16 girls in the most beautiful brand-new costumes. And there should have been major guest stars each week.

I persuaded Benny to play the first two weeks, although he had vowed never to work in the theatre again! The show and Benny were a sensation. So much for Bernie with Anne Shelton at the Alexandra Gardens! But that was it. A week of Arthur Askey, a lovely act but not a 'draw', a week of Eric Sykes and Hattie Jacques, first time together on stage and no act at all, a week of Alfred Marks and Freddie Mills the boxer, and finally Joe Baker and Jack Douglas. The audience got thinner and thinner and finally petered out. Anne Shelton was doing fine! I decided then that jealousy and ambition were not doing me any good. I was 40 years old, doing very nicely, and I had better settle for what I was, rather than striving to become Lord Stone.

The legendary Hollywood film-maker Hal Roach came to England. His mission was to find English comedians to remake his great Laurel and Hardy films. Someone must have sent him to me. We had a great time together. I drove him all over England to see the comics in summer shows, from Great Yarmouth to Newquay. He was such a lovely old man that even when it dawned on me that nothing would ever come of his dream, I drove on. Incidentally, in one of his angrier moments with the Colonel, Benny Hill accused me of never having introduced him to anyone interesting except Hal Roach.

Another American legend, Otto Preminger, was in London casting his latest picture. He needed two English comedy actors for a cameo. Maud Spector, the doyen of the casting directors, gathered the cream of English comedy to be interviewed by the great man in his suite at the Dorchester. The hotel lobby was littered with comedians and Maud called them up one by one. When it came to Terry Scott and Hugh Lloyd, they went in together. Otto Preminger sat behind a massive desk at the far end of his huge sitting room. There was only one chair, which naturally Terry sat upon. Hugh stood quietly at the back. Preminger said that he was looking for two removal men, and had been told that Terry and Hugh were starring in a television series. Did that mean, he asked, that they always had to work together? To which Hugh boldly replied, 'If the furniture is heavy, we certainly prefer to.'

They did not get the job.

Norman Vaughan had been a client and friend from very early on, and 1962 was his year. I remember one Christmas in the early years, booking

him for pantomime at Worthing and taking the family for the first performance on Boxing Day. We drove down in the old Morris with a picnic, to
save the price of lunch, and ate our sandwiches in a bus shelter on
Worthing front in the freezing cold! At one time Norman had my job with
Clarkson Rose in Twinkle. (There was another comedian in Twinkle, one
Billy Burden, a rustic raconteur from Dorset. He had been with Twinkle
for many years without a contract. When the show finished its tour each
December, Clarkie said to Billy, 'Rehearsals start next March. See you
then.' And Billy turned up. When Billy decided eventually that it was time
to move on, I became his agent and was deputed to break the news to
Clarkie!)

Norman was playing Blackpool when Val Parnell happened to be in
front. As a result of this lucky chance he succeeded Bruce Forsyth on
Sunday Night at the Palladium. He remained loyal, despite threats from
the Grade office that if he didn't leave Richard Stone and join them he
wouldn't get the job. For a time he was our biggest earner and, I think, the
first star to earn huge money from commercials ('Roses grow on you').
Benny was the next, advertising Schweppes until the commercials became
such one-minute comedy gems that they were promoting Benny and not
the product. Later, when things were not going well for Norman, I took
him out to lunch and told him, as an old friend, that if he felt a change of
agent would do him any good, I would not be at all hurt.

'Richard,' he replied, 'changing agents at this stage in my career would
be like changing deck chairs on the *Titanic*.'

How often Clarkson Rose seems to crop up in my early days. Tom
Mennard was a bus driver in Hove when he auditioned and was accepted
by Vivian Van Damm for the Windmill. There was quite a bit of publicity.
Clarkie rang to enquire about Tom and asked his salary. I told him Tom
was getting £40 a week at the Windmill. There was a long pause, and
Clarkie said, 'I'll ring you back.'

When he rang back he had done his homework. 'If Mr Mennard is
getting forty pounds at the Windmill, he is giving six shows a day for six
days, that's thirty-six shows. That works out at a little over a pound a
performance. We only do ten shows a week, so if I paid him fifteen pounds
a week, that would be a nice rise!'

Dear Clarkie.

Margate was to become my favourite date but we started at Margate in a
very small way. Basil Brown decided to put a touring show into the Butlin
hotels at Margate and Brighton and entrusted it to me. I had to buy a mini
bus to take the artistes between the two hotels. We bought one for £30 and
proudly painted *Richard Stone Productions* along the side. The comedians
were a double act, Daly and Wayne; Paddy Wayne drove the bus.
Unfortunately on one journey the windscreen fell right out, which, it

transpires, is a serious offence. When Mr Daly's evidence was read out in court, it contained the great excuse, 'It's not my fault, it's Richard Stone's fault.'

We also took over for two seasons Reg Varney and Benny's old pitch, the Lido. The first season did not start too well. Our star, Jimmy Wheeler ('Ay ay that's your lot') had been imbibing a little too freely all day. He made his first entrance, fell straight into the orchestra pit and paraphrased his well-known catchphrase, 'Ay ay, that's *my* lot!' But he was a dear man and when the season was obviously losing money, he offered to take a cut in salary. I have only been in receipt of this kind of gesture twice in my whole career. (For the record, the other time it was from Freddie 'Parrot-Face' Davies, who I was delighted to see recently giving a smashing performance in the film *Hear My Song*.)

The next year at the Lido we starred Bill Maynard and Joan Turner, who managed to make a 10-minute domestic sketch run for 40 minutes! Joan had the line 'I hope you'll be veeery comfortable', which she and Bill repeated and repeated to the delight of the holidaymakers, but even more to their mutual amusement, especially if Joan had had a couple.

I brought the American impressionist Frank Gorshin to England and persuaded the BBC to give him his own show. The first hold-up was an argument with the Musician's Union, who would not let Gorshin's American musical director conduct. This dispute wasted five hours so he never rehearsed. The studio audience assembled at seven o'clock. The director had decided that as most of the people being impersonated were dead, he would set the show in heaven. Unfortunately the smoke machine went mad and instead of providing a reasonable cloud effect, it immersed Frank Gorshin and the audience in a thick fog. When the fog cleared it was nine o'clock and the audience had gone home! My son Tim and I were the only two left for the recording, and much 'dubbed' laughter needed to be added.

I booked an unknown Dave Allen for eight weeks in Australia. He stayed two years and became a star down under with his own television series. He was contracted to a lovely bluff ex-policeman, Jack Neary, but he became friendly with his director and another Australian conman. They both subsequently took him for considerable rides, but it takes a lot to shake Dave's loyalty and he clung to them, much to my annoyance and to the detriment of his own pocket! He came back to England for a holiday and I fixed him a date on *Sunday Night at the London Palladium*. When he finally came home he was given a regular slot on the Val Doonican shows, and was a star in England as well!

David Croft was now at the BBC and, in 1968, he and Jimmy Perry wrote the pilot script for *Dad's Army*. It was turned down by the then Controller of BBC1, Paul Fox, as being too 'beastly to the Germans'. But a great Head of Light Entertainment, Tom Sloane, overruled him and the pilot was made. Tom was not of show business, but he knew what the public wanted – we could do with a few Tom Sloanes in television today. After the phenomenal success of *Dad's Army,* David went on to co-write *Are You Being Served?*, *It Ain't Arf Ot, Mum, Hi-de-Hi!,* and *'Allo 'Allo!* But, not only did he co-write these shows, he was also the producer and director. Such a phenomenal string of successes put David in a unique position in British television. In America, where almost every show has an army of writers, producers and directors, he would never be allowed to function as he did here. He was an employee of the BBC as a contract producer, but such was his track record that he told the BBC what, where, when and how he was going to produce his next success. The 'where' made sure that all the location shooting, whether jungle, the battlefields of France, or a holiday camp, was done near his home at Bury-St-Edmunds.

Jimmy Perry, Bill Roberton and I organised a surprise lunch for David a few years ago. He thought he was coming to meet an Australian impresario, but when I took him into the hotel, some 150 actors, studio managers and technicians who had worked with him over the years were waiting to pay their respects, and they had all happily paid for their own lunch! David wrote mainly with two people. Jimmy Perry came up with the ideas for *Dad's Army, It Ain't Arf Ot, Mum* and *Hi-de-Hi!* – based on his own experiences in the Home Guard, in Burma, and as a Butlin's Redcoat. Jimmy was great on situation and plot. In my opinion these three are the 'classiest' but Jimmy was a perfectionist and it took them a long time to write a script. So David turned sometimes to Jeremy Lloyd and they wrote the funny *Are you Being Served?* and *'Allo 'Allo!* packed with one-liners, very quickly.

With David's background it is not surprising that he became a master showman. The son of a musical comedy Star, Anne Croft, he grew up in the business. Actor, singer, lyric writer and finally producer, director and writer of television hits for over 40 years, David had the uncanny knack of selecting a team of relatively unknowns for each show. Within a year, they considered themselves stars. But it's the writers who were really the stars for creating the roles which made them national figures. A few exceptions had star quality aside from their TV image, but very few. Within a year of the end of the series most began to slip back whence they came, and one noted member of the cast of *It Ain't Arf Ot, Mum* actually blamed David and Jimmy for his one brief hour of glory! *Sic transit gloria.* Their series have been made into films and stage shows but probably because of their subject matter never hit it off in America – until *Are You Being Served?* became a huge cult success on Public Broadcasting, even on occasions being shown all evening.

The 1960s were expanding years for our summer shows. Worthing was a small but worthwhile date, for the season ran from April until October. It was a conservative stronghold and considered itself rather 'posh'. I therefore decided to apply for the date as Colonel Stone. Each year the *Worthing Herald* carried a banner headline: 'Colonel Stone announces his plans for this year's Summer Show', which always struck me as being rather a heavy-weight announcement for a small concert party.

Diana was at school at Battle Abbey near Hastings. I don't know what the other girls did on their days out but poor Diana sat and watched dress rehearsals in the circle at the White Rock Pavilion, Hastings. By the mid-sixties we had ten resident shows, employing some 60 stars and supporting acts and nearly a hundred chorus girls wearing, with various changes of programme, over 1,800 costumes. I was also booking early seasons and Sunday concerts into five resorts. Bill Roberton helped me sort out and book the acts. When we had fixed the 'top', Bill would exclaim, 'All we need now is sixpennyworth of Bassett's.' [Bassett's being Liquorice All-sorts and Bill referring to the supporting artistes.]

From all our shows and concerts the manager sent a telegram, in code, each night giving the day's takings. We used for the code the name of a very co-operative chorus girl, one Norma Lewis, so that the letters of her name represent the figures from 0–9. Terry Scott was heading a very early season variety bill in Scarborough, sometime in May. Doubling as Touring Manager, he phoned the Scarborough operator with the figure for the night's takings to be wired to London – 'Scarborough Monday First House N.M., Second house R.O.'

'Oh,' said the operator. 'You're not doing very well, dear, are you.'

A similar thing happened to Louis Benjamin, later to be Managing Director of Moss Empires, when as a very young theatre manager he was posted to Morecambe. It was difficult to find inexpensive attractions to keep this vast theatre open in the winter months. So Val Parnell, his boss in London, authorised Louis to pay small guarantees to touring plays. One week the play opened very badly.

Val was enraged. 'Why are you paying a three hundred pound guarantee and playing to five pounds on Monday and three pounds on Tuesday?'

And Louis' classic reply was, 'I'm sorry, Mr Parnell, but the takings always go down on a Tuesday.'

A week after the encounter with the Scarborough telephone operator, Terry and Hugh were topping for me at Bridlington and Russ Conway was topping at Scarborough. Russ complained of nerves and that his fingers were refusing to move. I phoned Terry to rearrange the running order in Bridlington, so that he could drive the 30 miles up the road and be prepared to double with Scarborough. When he arrived backstage Russ was at the piano, his hands about to freeze. However, when he saw Terry hovering in the wings they unfroze very quickly, and he launched into a spirited rendering of 'Side-Saddle'. I heard Russ on the radio before he was a top of the bill and a huge draw. I booked him for several early season variety bills at, I think, £75 a week. Then came 'Side-Saddle'. At Torquay our top was Bob Monkhouse, in those days a name but sadly never a draw. I think his fee was about £500 on account of a large percentage which I never thought he'd get. But Russ Conway packed the theatre for £75 and Bob came out with over £1,000.

The year before Leslie Henson died Sara was in a play with him at Windsor. Leslie made me promise to keep an eye out for his son. It was on a visit to Charterhouse that I first saw Nicky appearing in a play with our son Barry and I became his agent at once. Nicky never went to drama school, his first job was as front man on a teenage magazine show at Tyne-Tees TV. He also told me recently that I offered him the job of being the first male vocalist in Ivy Benson's all girl band – but I don't believe him! He formed a group, the Wombats, with Ian Ogilvy and Stanley Holloway's son Julian. Despite this unconventional start he's done pretty well professionally over the years. And as well as his wives Una Stubbs and the ballerina Marguerite Porter, he's bedded quite a selection of nice ladies.

One of my happiest memories of Nicky concerns a film producer, Lindsay Shonteff, one of the small-time greats. Lindsay made films on a shoestring budget with his wife carrying out most of the functions of production manager, wardrobe, sets and costumes. He shot his films without permission in the streets of London, until the police moved him on. He engaged Nicky to play a poor man's James Bond, Charles Bind, 'number one' of the Secret Service. He was asked if he had a dinner jacket, and he hadn't. So Lindsay took him to a second-hand tailor in Tottenham Court Road, where they selected a DJ, priced at £10. Lindsay disappeared into the back of the shop. When he emerged no money had passed. He had got the dinner jacket for nothing in exchange for a screen credit! I booked not only Nicky into this film, but Richard Todd as 'M' and Aimi Macdonald as the love interest. They were offered such appalling salaries that I asked for generous percentages. He gave me 25 per cent of his share of the British box office for each of them. It seemed an incredibly generous gesture to be giving away 75 per cent. Too late I found out that Lindsay made his films for the Far East and they were never ever shown in England!

In 1964 things were not going well for Ian Carmichael. After several hit shows in London we picked on a stinker. I had met, in New York, Lynne Loesser, the ex-wife of Frank Loesser. She was trying to set up, for London, a musical based on Molière's *Le Malade Imaginaire*, called *The Love Doctor*. It was written by Forest and Wright, who had created *Kismet*. Lynne was prepared to put up half the capital and wanted an English co-producer. She was very keen to get Ian Carmichael to star, and also another client of mine, Joan Heal. Joan had been a considerable leading lady in the West End since her early success in *Grab me a Gondola*. Ian and Joan both liked the show. I took it to Robert Morley and his agent Robin Fox, who had recently set up in management together and had had a success with Ian in *The Tunnel of Love*. Robert claimed to know nothing about musicals, and I don't think was really very impressed with the show. When we played him the score, he lay flat on his back on the floor of his office, apparently asleep. However, as Ian wanted to do it, and Forest and Wright had written it, they agreed to co-present in London.

The first disaster was that Lynne Loesser failed to come up with her half of the money. The second disaster was that although Forest and Wright had written a pleasant enough score, there were no really good songs. Perhaps we had all chosen to forget that Borodin wrote *Kismet*! The third disaster was that the opening night in Manchester revealed a very inadequate 'book'. Panic set in as it always does on these occasions, and a new writer was flown from Hollywood. Wendy Toye was secretly engaged to jolly it up but the American director was not to know! She was to lurk at the back of the theatre in dark glasses. In Oxford, Robin Fox was in tears as he, rightly, foresaw the sad end of his production company. I last saw Forest and Wright outside the New Theatre, hailing a taxi to start their journey back to New York. Nothing could save the show.

It was Ian's first big flop. His film career was also coming to an end. It was in no way Ian's fault. He had been Britain's number one comedy star when comedy films were being made. There just weren't those sort of films any more. I begged Ian to go into television, Michael Mills had asked him to play Bertie Wooster in a forthcoming BBC Wodehouse series. But like so many film stars of the day, he considered television to be a second-rate medium. So we chased a rainbow. The rainbow ended in a small studio in Copenhagen in a low-budget, totally unfunny, Danish-English co-production.

It was nevertheless a terrible shock when I received, at Seaview in the summer, a kind but nevertheless final letter from Ian terminating our relationship as client and agent. Emotionally this was the worst moment of my career. It was like a divorce. Ian had been my staff captain at Thirty Corps. He had been my best friend in the immediate post-war years. He had lived with Sara and me at St George's Terrace. I was godfather to his second daughter. We had planned all those early summer shows together. I know it hurt him too, and his book, *Will the Real Ian Carmichael . . .*, is a tribute to our friendship. When he left, the first job he accepted was Bertie Wooster on television, and his career recovered and took on a new dimension. *C'est la vie!*

In the 1960s, when our children were teenagers, number 7 St George's Terrace became the favourite free accommodation in London. We had so many rooms and the house went up so high, that some of our children's friends were with us for months at a time. I met a charming young woman not so long ago in California. She claimed to know me well from a six-month stay with us in London, but was not surprised that I didn't remember her. She had apparently lived in a room at the top of the house, and was not sure if we knew she was there! When we moved to a smaller house in 1972 we winkled out the lodgers from the various corners and explained to them that their time was up.

I met Francis Essex when, as a mere lad, he had somehow scraped together the money to mount a revue at the St Martins Theatre called appropriately *The Bells of St Martins*. Our client Hattie Jacques had been one of the stars. Francis and I became friends. He was a keen sailor. We used to go for weekends to Gosport, where he kept his first Westerley, and sail in the Solent. He was doubtful about my devotion to sailing. He claimed that as we came out of Portsmouth harbour, I was much too interested in trying to count the queue on Southsea Pier for my summer show starring Terry Scott and Hugh Lloyd, when I should have been concentrating on keeping close to the wind!

Terry came over one Sunday to the Isle of Wight and I took him out in our dinghy. It was quite windy, so I explained that, on the command 'ready about', he was to move his not inconsiderable weight, to the other side of the boat. This he failed to do and we capsized, not, I may say, more than 50 yards from the shore. Tim was playing on the beach and soon had some-one out to rescue us. But Terry's publicity agent, Margot Lovell, was also on holiday on the island. Never one to miss an opportunity, she phoned the press. One tabloid the next day carried a headline, 'Terry Scott in Solent Drama'!

When Barry left Charterhouse he went on to study art at Corsham. Afterwards he travelled with a donkey all through Yugoslavia and, being wrongly accused of stealing the donkey, spent a night in a Turkish jail. When he came back from his travels, I fixed him a job as a trainee researcher with Scottish Television, where Francis Essex was now Programme Controller. His research was not meant to take him to a deserted island off the west coast, but this is where he went with Eric Newby's daughter Sonia – travel must have been in her blood. Poor Francis was distraught. He thought something ghastly had happened to his agent's eldest son, who had been put into his care. He had Barry's dis-appearance announced on the screen during the local news. After teaching English in a girl's school in Seville, an abortive attempt to study architec-ture at Toronto University, 'finding himself' with primal therapy and nearly killing himself hang-gliding, he finally drifted into the film industry. It was a long and difficult ride for us, and I suspect, for him. He hadn't liked us much or thanked us for a conventional upbringing. But we

97

hung in, and now we are the best of friends, and Barry is getting excellent work as a director of photography and winning awards all over the world.

We had progressed from Ford Consuls to a tank-like convertible Mercedes. We shipped this monster on a plane from Lydd to Le Touquet – I believe this ferry only ran for a couple of years, it was probably uneconomical as it only carried four cars! We drove to Montreux, where one of Benny's shows was the BBC entry for the 'Golden Rose'. This is the only time in my career that I have attended this junket for the entire TV light entertainment world. It nearly ended in disaster when, coming back down a steep and winding hill to the Palace Hotel after a party with the Mercedes piled high with VIPs, Eric Maschwitz's wife Phyllis, even more sloshed than usual, suddenly threw a mackintosh over my head, totally blinding me on a particularly dangerous bend!

We had a show in Southend in 1965, starring Jimmy Edwards and Joan Regan. We were rather particular about our finales, providing beautiful gowns for the chorus, and superior matching ones for the lady principals. We did, however, expect the men to have a dinner jacket. It was a slight shock therefore to learn, at the dress rehearsal, that Jimmy had not brought his along. He offered to fly himself home to collect it but a thick fog descended. Fortunately the mayor had a similarly ample figure and Jimmy walked down in the finale on the opening night in the mayor's dinner jacket! Joan Regan was popular but was inclined to stay on rather a long time singing all her hits. Hugh Lloyd went to see the show. I asked him the next day what Joan Regan had in her act.

'Everything – except an Interval!'

Pickwick with music by Cyril Ornadel, had a good run in London with Harry Secombe as Mr Pickwick. It was presented by Bernard Delfont. As in all West End play contracts, there was an option for the management to present, or sublet, the show in New York. Bernie's office had never taken up the option, so that when David Merrick decided to transfer the show to Broadway, we did our own deal with Merrick. We asked, on behalf of everyone concerned, music, lyrics and book, the usual ten per cent. Merrick went mad. Our American lawyer took the negotiations to the edge of the cliff and issued an injunction to stop the show opening in Philadelphia. Merrick climbed down and agreed to pay ten per cent for the tour, but a much lesser percentage in New York. The show toured for six months to capacity and cost Merrick a lot of money in royalties. It didn't make the grade on Broadway and saved him very little. Merrick, not the most popular of impresarios, was so angry by then that he didn't attend the first night. He was in Vietnam with Ginger Rogers! He gave, but did not attend, the most uninviting first night party in what seemed to me to be a roped-off section of a Lyons Corner House!

Tony Sympson was a diminutive, smiling pixie of a man, with an enormous white beard, and was quite wealthy. With his two similar pixie brothers, he virtually owned the whole of Goodwins Court, a picturesque alley leading off St Martins Lane. He advertised in *The Stage*: 'Tony Sympson, Character Actor, salary £27 10s.' However, he came to me to negotiate a more reasonable salary for the American tour of *Pickwick*, remained with me for life, and never worked for £27 10s again! When he was in *Fiddler on the Roof* he was not only a major investor in the show, but was also landlord to the management, who had their office in Goodwins Court. Nevertheless, Tony would come every Friday to our office to make sure his weekly salary cheque had arrived.

Sara and I went on from New York for a holiday in the Bahamas. Whilst we were there we inspected a development on the island of Little Exuma. We earmarked our plot, which, although slightly swampy, was on the beach in a location that we were promised would be developed as the yacht harbour. We came home to London and paid the estate agents who were promoting the scheme, £400. When we next went to the Bahamas, the sales team had disappeared. Soon the estate agents closed in London. I fear our plot is still a swamp, and would not set much store by our deed of ownership!

The 1960s saw the birth of the then daring TV show *That Was The Week That Was*. It was live on a Saturday night, topical and controversial. My connection with the show was Lance Percival. Lance sang an impromptu calypso based on the week's events and became quite famous. I remember booking him an almost impossible schedule. He started his day at 6 a.m. on a film set. At about 6 p.m. he drove like the clappers to Bournemouth, where he was appearing in Harold Fielding's *Music for the Millions*. At about 10.30 p.m. he drove from Bournemouth back to London for his night club engagement at 2 a.m. and so back to the film set at 6 a.m.! Lance had a hit record with 'Shame and Scandal in the Family', a West Indian calypso. On a recent holiday in St Lucia I heard it sung 40 years later by two local entertainers.

Dave Allen was one of the first British acts to be offered a spot on the *Ed Sullivan Show*. We went together and on the Thursday, prior to the Sunday recording, Dave submitted his script to the producer, Ed Sullivan's son-in-law with the unfortunate surname of Pricht. The script was accepted. When we came for the run-through in an empty studio on the Sunday morning Ed watched from the control room. Dave and I were sent for after the run-through and were told that the material was not suitable for his family audience. But Pricht had accepted it four days before. Most pros would have eaten humble pie and found another script. Not Dave. He walked out! On a cold, wintry Sunday morning in New York, Dave and I sat eating doughnuts and drinking coffee. We had come 3,000 miles for nothing. But it was I who was distraught, Dave was totally philosophical about the whole affair.

He showed the same spirit when he was booked for a week's cabaret at the Savoy Hotel. After the first night I received, by hand, a letter from Freddie Lloyd, the managing director of the Savoy, instructing Dave to take out all references to sex, religion and politics. He went on for his appearance on the Tuesday, read out the letter and walked off!

When Tim was a little boy and Barry had said that one day it would be 'Richard Stone & Son', Tim had piped up with 'Richard Stone & Son & Bros'', so I was thrilled when he joined the office. I had just broken up with Felix. We had been together for over 20 years, and had known each other since before the war. The agency was doing well but I was producing 90 per cent of the income for 50 per cent the of the profits! Felix, I thought, was away from the office far too much, handling the affairs of one John Marshall, who I mistrusted and disliked intensely. When John came into the office he behaved as if he was the third partner and treated our petty cash and the staff accordingly. I suggested banning John Marshall from the building and a new 20-year partnership on a 60/40 basis. Felix declined on both counts. I would dearly love to have been friends again but Felix has, I'm afraid, remained sore.

Danny la Rue was in those days primarily a night club performer. Apart from pantomime, he had not been seen by a wider public. It was Sara who thought that he would be equally successful in a summer show. Danny was prepared to have a go, but was not willing to leave his club. We therefore had to persuade the Margate Corporation to go 'once nightly' so that Danny could commute to London after the show. It was a complete sellout. So much so that Danny came to have great confidence in us. We met in the pub, on the corner of St George's Terrace in the autumn, and Danny asked if we would like to present him in London. But I was not a West End impresario, nor had I any financial backers. I decided to seek a partner, and who better than Michael Codron. Michael was enthusiastic. He had *Not Now Darling* about to finish a long run at the Strand, which would be an ideal theatre for Danny. We were just about to set out for a holiday in November when Michael phoned me to say that he was very sorry but he didn't think this sort of show was his cup of tea after all, and he wished to withdraw. It was two days before we were due to fly to New York. I rushed around to see Ray Cooney, the author of *Not Now Darling*, who had just begun to spread his wings as an impresario. Regrettably, Danny, or maybe his agent, Sonny Zahl, didn't reckon that Ray was a suitable replacement for Michael Codron and, with no more time on my side, I lost my chance to become a West End producer and went on holiday.

It made sense to move the scenery and costumes of our shows to a new

100

resort each year. If the same artistes were available this was a bonus as it cut production costs to a minimum. They fitted the costumes, and used the same orchestrations.

But Danny was not prepared to go all the way to Scarborough so we sent our glamorous show there, but starring Tommy Cooper! Freddie Carpenter, the director, might have compromised a little, but no, for the finale he had Tommy Cooper walk down a long flight of steps, not actually in Danny's dress but singing, oh so slowly, Noël Coward's 'The Party's Over Now'.

After the first night Freddie returned to town, leaving an embarrassed and somewhat enraged Tommy Cooper. Next day I cut the walk down and the song and substituted a quick curtain call!

We came down most weekends to the Isle of Wight, where we had bought a holiday flat. I amused myself composing limericks about the places we went through, and I remember two of them:

> A conjuror at Forest Mere
> turned out to be terribly queer.
> With the aid of a carrot
> he buggered the parrot
> then made the poor bird disappear.

> There was a young bride from Cowplain
> who kept coming again and again.
> But her husband the vicar
> came once and much quicker
> which gave her much cause to complain.

Moira Lister, otherwise the Vicomtesse D'Orthez, is a mixture of actress and society hostess. Many times I have brought impresarios who might give her a job to her magnificent flat in Cadogan Square, only for them to feel after a glass of D'Orthez champagne that it is they who are being interviewed! A visit to the villa on the Cape D'Ail was another rare treat. But get her working and there isn't a more conscientious, hard-working old pro around. She was starring in a courtroom drama *A Woman Called Anne*, which opened at the Lyceum, Edinburgh. So delighted was the director of the theatre to have Moira Lister and a prior-to-London play grace their boards that he built the scenery and made the costumes and gave them to the management, free gratis and for nothing. The management, Henry Sherwood, then sold the production to the backers of the West End show for £15,000!

Whilst the show was in Brighton, we all went to Plumpton race course to see the first racehorse of which we owned a leg, in a syndicate with dear

Felix Bowness. It came in at 25 to 1. We have been in racehorse syndicates ever since!

In the late sixties Benny Hill left the BBC, lured by Lew Grade to take part in some Anglo-American variety shows. The shows had American stars, producers and directors and were in every way, and especially for Benny, a disaster. I remember, as we drove back from Elstree after the last recording, Benny said, 'We shall never drive this way again.'

Benny could have gone back to the BBC but I think he was scared of getting into a rut and being regarded as part of the furniture. He wanted a change and so I advised him to sign with Thames, where he made as many as seven and as few as two shows a year for nearly 20 years. Philip Jones, the Head of Light Entertainment for every year except the last, was quite the best and nicest light entertainment boss in television.

Barry Took, after Benny's death, wrote a book about Benny and Frankie Howerd. He filled a lot of space with inter-office memos and letters, so perhaps I may learn a lesson and quote a letter he quoted!

Richard Stone Esq.   18th June 1969
13/20 York Buildings
Adelphi
WC2

Dear Richard

I am quite shattered to hear that Benny Hill has been contracted to appear in a series for one of our competitors.

Shattered not because I really expect loyalty in an affair like this – but because at no time have I been asked to make any sort of counter offer – and this after 15 years of the closest association with yourself and Benny. Admittedly I have always taken Benny on trust – but this has always been your wish that we should not attempt to contract him whilst he was still so firmly involved in films.

I accepted the shows in colour for ATV without a great deal of protest because I hoped it might further Benny's career in the United States. When we booked him for the four shows in 1969, I accepted your demand that they should be repeated because, as you put it 'It was important for Benny to be seen on television this year'.

Unless I am a very simple lad, I read this as meaning that it was in both our interest to keep Benny before our public until he can do some more shows for us.

You really do not expect me now to set up an audience for Thames Television by actually transmitting these?

I consider your action in not allowing us to even make Benny an offer has released me from any obligation to actually run these repeats. I am therefore going to ask our Contracts Department to make the appropriate payments in lieu.

Yours sincerely

Tom Sloane, Head of Entertainment Group Television.

I loved Tom and have paid homage to him elsewhere in this book. I understand his annoyance as a loyal servant of the BBC, but I don't think it was really justified. Benny was not under contract, nor had he made any promises to go back to the BBC.

10

J.B. Priestley comes to see Fred Emney, the end of my summer shows, David Jason's first success, Derek Nimmo and Bill Maynard come to blows, and Victoria Wood spreads her wings

The 1970s saw the end of our summer seasons and the start of two new relationships.

The first was with a lady client. I suppose approaching 50 is a dangerous age. However, this pleasurable interlude lasted only a few months and no great harm was done.

The second relationship was more stable and has lasted longer. Paul Elliot put on one of his first shows, a production of *Boeing Boeing*, on the South Parade Pier, Blackpool. Blackpool boasted three piers, North, Central and South. The theatre on the South Parade Pier was the White Elephant. Paul had virtually rented the venue from April until October. I begged him to think again, being convinced that what he was paying in April and May was twice as much as he would be taking at the box office and that he would be broke before June, when the season *might* begin to perk up. My gloom was justified, and it looked as if *Boeing Boeing* might have to come off after only two weeks. We decided to send the formidable Bill Dickie to beard the pier company directors.

I would like to have been a fly on the wall at that meeting. Apparently he opened the proceedings by announcing in his best stentorian tones, 'I represent Richard Stone of London!' A fact which I am sure fell on deaf Lancastrian ears. He then lambasted them for doing such a tough deal with a young and inexperienced impresario. Having reduced them to tears of shame, he came away with the entire deal reversed, and with Paul receiving a handsome weekly guarantee from the theatre!

When Paul teamed up with Duncan Weldon I was already a bit of a fairy godfather. Their first West End show together was a revival of Priestley's *When We Are Married*. I cast for them Peggy Mount, Hugh Lloyd and Daphne Anderson, and then thought how wonderful Fred Emney would be as the drunken photographer. There was no difficulty in getting Duncan and Paul to accept him. Fred was the problem. He was used to leading roles and top billing! The show opened in Guildford, directed by Laurier Lister. Laurier was a delightful old thing, the long-time partner of Max Adrian, and had made his name directing rather gentle, intimate revues. He was a little shattered by Fred, who saw no reason to stick strictly to the words of Priestley. During the rehearsals, when given rather complicated moves, Fred asked if he could have a map! By the time the show opened, Fred had prevailed upon Laurier to allow him to sit at the piano and entertain with one of his own songs! He had a wonderful bit of business settling down at the piano stool with a cushion, which he eventually threw away with the line, 'Never could stand heights!'

Paul tells that by way of conversation he remarked to Fred that he thought he had lost a little weight. To which Fred replied, 'Yes, I've given up mint sauce.'

Priestley himself came to the dress rehearsal. Afterwards Laurier told the artistes to wait while he discussed their performances with Mr Priestley, then he would come back stage with Priestley's notes. Fred sat puffing on his cigar. Peggy Mount asked him, with her usual modesty, if he were not worried about what the great man might think of it all.

'Good God, no. If he didn't think it was funny, he shouldn't have written the bloody thing.'

The show and Fred got good notices. Brian Hewitt-Jones however, playing the small part of the Vicar received only one notice: 'Vicars are sometimes ridiculous but never as ridiculous as Mr Hewitt-Jones. Brian has wisely given up acting and was, until recently, a director of Paul Elliot's production company!

Two more Emney stories. A fellow star comedian, the late Bobby Howes, was arrested for indecent exposure. When Fred heard about it he said, 'Poor old Bobby waving it about. I can't even find mine!'

And my last memory of Fred is sad but typical. Duncan and Paul were reviving *A Funny Thing Happened on the Way to the Forum* and bringing over their first major American star to play the lead. Phil Silvers, who had by now suffered two strokes, arrived at London Airport to be met by an effusive Duncan.

'Mr Silvers, it is an honour to be presenting you in England. Is there anything I can do for you?'

'Yes, give me the other half of my ticket and put me on a plane back to Los Angeles.'

It didn't bode well, and Fred Emney, who incongruously was playing the almost silent but show-stopping part originally played in London by the diminutive Robertson Hare, hated Phil Silvers on sight. The show opened at the Forum Theatre, Billingham. This was a terrible date.

Billingham, in the Tyne Tees area, is an isolated industrial town. Its theatre could only attract good shows by heavy subsidy. It became a Mecca for struggling managements who got their scenery and costumes made, and the show mounted for nothing in return for a nebulous interest in future profits. For the artistes it was hell. Cold and miserable, with one pub, the Billingham Arms, as their accommodation. No wonder Phil Silvers, a sick man from sunny California, and Fred Emney, an old man from the Savoy Hotel, London, were not in a good mood.

After the dress rehearsal Fred said his chihuahua was ill at his house in Bognor, and left! He quoted a clause in his Equity contract that stipulated he was due two weeks' holiday in every year, so he was taking it now! Duncan and Paul wanted to sue him but I persuaded them to forget it and they quickly booked Arnold Ridley (of *Dad's Army*) to replace him. Two weeks later the show was playing the Theatre on the Green at Richmond, Surrey. This obviously appealed a little more to Fred. On the Monday he rang the box office to ask what time the curtain went up.

'Why do you want to know, sir?'

'I'm Fred Emney, I'm in it. I've been on holiday.'

Dear old Fred. I'm afraid he didn't get his part back.

By 1970 our summer shows were petering out. The seaside holiday in England was not so popular, and everyone was going abroad. The smaller dates like Worthing and Hastings could no longer support a show, and in some cases the theatres had already become bingo halls. We were left with Scarborough, Margate and the Butlin camps. It was becoming increasingly difficult to find stars willing to play a long season but we were lucky that year to have Mike and Bernie Winters for Margate, and Bob Monkhouse for Scarborough. As Bob was currently on television in *The Golden Shot*, with a fantastic touch of imagination we called our show *The Golden Show* and spent a fortune on golden scenery, golden dresses and a mass of gold sequins all over the tabs. With Bob, a relatively unknown and therefore inexpensive Les Dawson, and Ronnie Hilton, we thought we had a winner. The local papers praised it as our best show ever, but it did no business and we lost the date.

With only Margate left, 1971 was the bottom, I simply could not find a good box office attraction. We finished up with Mary Hopkin, who had had a couple of hit records, and Lonnie Donegan, a good performer but no longer box office. My star told me that she would not be satisfied with the brilliant Betty Smith Quintet that had accompanied all our shows in Margate for eight years. She wanted a 12-piece orchestra. After all that, she turned up at the dress rehearsal with two odd-looking gypsies with violins and no band parts for the expensive orchestra she had ordered. Furthermore she had no dress for her act and we had to belt around Margate buying her something to wear.

STONE MERGING SUMMER ACTIVITIES

Joining forces with Elliott and Weldon

Due to the rapid expansion of his agency and his involvement in television and film packaging, RICHARD STONE (left) has decided to merge his future summer season activities with PAUL ELLIOTT and DUNCAN C. WELDON.

Elliott and Weldon will have the benefit of the Companies wardrobe department and the entire stock of costumes and scenery. Although all contracts in future will be handled by Elliott and Weldon they will be able to call on Richard Stone and his staff as technical advisors.

In more than 20 years Richard Stone has presented over 150 shows in almost every seaside resort in the country. In earlier years the shows either starred or helped build the careers of his own clients, including BENNY HILL, DAVE ALLEN, TERRY SCOTT, HUGH LLOYD, JON PERTWEE, BILL MAYNARD, LANCE PERCIVAL, TOM MENNARD, BILLY BURDEN, BOBBY DENNIS and FELIX BOWNESS.

I decided enough was enough and it was time to get out. I gave my costumes and scenery to Duncan and Paul. In 24 years we had presented over 150 shows in almost every seaside resort in the country.

Charles Vance took over Margate and booked Norman Vaughan. Charles is the personification of the actor manager Johnnie. He wears a green velvet jacket with satin revers and affects a walking stick. He is the president of this and that and writes articles in *The Stage*. He had a very good repertory company in Weston-super-Mare when we had the summer shows there. I think Margate was his first ever summer show and it was terrible. I had come to see Norman and was lurking at the back of the first night party when Charles was making his speech. Pointing at me, he announced, at his mellifluous and theatrical best, 'There is the man who taught me all I know about summer shows.'

A wag whispered rather too loudly, 'Well, you couldn't have been listening.'

In 1971 Moira Lister had her greatest success in the theatre in *Move Over Mrs Markham*. The play was written by Ray Cooney and John Chapman, and presented by Peter Saunders. It opened its short prior-to-London tour at Southsea. On the Saturday night I had a lot of telephone calls. The show was moving on to Brighton on the Sunday, and in those days artistes normally went by train, paid for by the management. Moira had mostly worked for the prestigious H.M. Tennants, who treated their stars with kid gloves and sent them first-class. (The powerful boss of H.M. Tennants, 'Binkie' Beaumont, was very camp. His offices were at the top of the Queens Theatre in Shaftesbury Avenue. You went up there in a very tiny lift. It was said that if a male actor was lucky enough to travel with 'Binkie' his future was secure.) To get back to Peter, he was a stickler for the rules, claiming that the Equity agreement only demanded third-class fares, and indeed he had recently sat on a committee to negotiate this very point! The difference between first and third on the short journey to Brighton cannot have been more than a couple of shillings, but Peter was adamant. Moira was incensed but eventually left Southsea. It helped somewhat that Cicely Courtneidge, the other major name in the show, had accepted the inevitable. Once he had made his point, Peter sent a dozen bottles of whisky to Moira's dressing room.

Bill Dickie's young brother, Murray, was a successful opera singer. He was by now a permanent member of the Vienna State Opera Company, and as their leading 'buffo' tenor had a fat salary paid for life. But Murray was a hustler and was always plying me with ideas that would make our fortune. One such idea was for a television series based on the Strauss family. I put the idea to Francis Essex, now Head of Production for Lew Grade. Francis wisely did not go into detail but described the series to Lew as, 'a *Forsyte Saga* with music'. We were in business. As Tommy Cooper would have said, 'Just like that.' Cyril Ornadel was brought in to arrange the music and to conduct the London Philharmonic Orchestra. By a glorious twist in the law, all the Strausses being dead and their music out of copyright, Cyril as the arranger, collected all the royalties for the music. It was one of Murray's better ideas and earned a few bob for us all.

David Croft's wife had been working in my office, and amongst the talent she had spotted was a young part-time actor and electrician, one David Jason. The struggling years are perhaps the most interesting in any career and David certainly struggled on the way to becoming probably the biggest box office attraction in British television. My first memory of David is taking the impresario John Gale to see him as Bob Acres in *The Rivals* at Sadlers Wells. John was looking for an actor to take over from Michael Crawford in the legendary *No Sex Please, We're British*. John, who reckoned that anyone who could be funny as Bob Acres could be funny anywhere, gave David the part. I was pleased to get him the work, any work, but foresaw disaster. Michael was a huge star and it seemed that to replace him with an unknown was a sure way to empty the theatre. But I had reckoned without David's comic genius. He brought a new dimension to the part, not to mention a lot of new funny business. The box office never wavered. David set a precedent for yearly 'takeovers' and the show ran for another 14 years.

108

In the next five years David starred in a couple of unsuccessful TV series and began his association with Ronnie Barker, playing Ronnie's nephew in *Open All Hours*. He adored Ronnie, learnt a lot from him and thought quite rightly that he was a master comic actor. David was known but hardly a star. I used his slight claim to fame to book him in summer season farces. He has been kind enough to thank me for getting him the work and for consistently bothering to visit him in far-flung and slightly seedy seaside pavilions. He was not so grateful when I persuaded him to take over from Terry Scott in a successful, but by now ailing farce, *A Bed Full of Foreigners*, which closed a few weeks later! His first and only pantomime was in Newcastle, playing Buttons in *Cinderella*. Neither he nor the director on loan from the more heady atmosphere of the local civic repertory theatre had any idea what pantomime was really about. I went to the dress rehearsal and witnessed a rather sombre fairytale weighed down with a ghastly script. David was getting very few laughs. Fortunately I am reasonably versed in the traditional pantomime 'wheezes' and spent some time persuading David to cut the dialogue and concentrate on throwing sweets to the children and other such delights. We introduced that popular 'bit' for the kids, where the comic, being chased by the ghost and thinking he is no longer behind him, utters the immortal words 'Oh no he isn't!' But the ghost is there and the kids (of course) shout back, 'Oh yes he is!' – no pantomime is complete without it.

David Jason took his pantomime punishment like a man and *Only Fools and Horses* followed in 1981 and the struggle was over. David is still with my office, although I have been retired for over ten years. I would say he is a contented man, not reaching for the moon, enjoying his success but not being surprised by it. He really is a very nice human being. I rang him after the transmission of *All the King's Men*, in which he gave a quite brilliant performance. He modestly accepted my congratulations and then thanked me as if I had made it happen.

I grew to love pantomime and its incongruities, such as the Cinderella picking up twigs in the forest and exclaiming, 'What have we here, an accordion?' and launching into her act! Or when Issy Bonn, the famous Jewish comedian, playing Abanazar, gives Aladdin one wish before he sends him into the cave to fetch the lamp, 'What I wish for,' wisely replies the unusually buxom lad (Barbara Windsor?) 'is to hear Issy Bonn sing "My Yiddisher Momma"!' Whereupon Issy throws off his robes, revealing his dinner jacket, and treats the audience to his famous signature tune.

I once visited a small provincial pantomime where, to close the first half, a decidedly camp Friar Tuck in Sherwood Forest sang 'Jerusalem' whilst the famous and expensive Curries Waterfalls inappropriately cascaded down behind him!

For many years all our clients, without the will to resist, were booked up and down the country in pantomime. Two distinguished members of the Royal Shakespeare Company, visiting the office in November to discuss with my more serious-minded, legitimate executive what they would do now that their contracts had expired, were pounced on by me, dragged into my office and found themselves teamed together as Captain and Mate in *Dick Whittington* at Hull! Bill Owen (Compo), who was with the office until he died, was another victim. Playwright, song-writer and splendid straight actor, Bill was game to try his hand at anything. Fortunately, his first pantomime was at Bromley with Dickie Henderson who taught him all the tricks. Thereafter Bill gave his Baron Hardup for Paul Elliot, who told me that Bill was his lucky mascot. Wherever he went each year the pantomime was a riot. A memorable Captain in *Dick Whittington* was an old friend and client, John Hewer. John, at the end of his career was making a comfortable living depicting a famous running character in a food commercial. Not wishing to prejudice his main source of income, we gave assurances that he would not bring their product into disrepute while appearing as Captain Birdseye in Aberdeen!

No longer running shows, the early 1970s saw me taking life a bit easier. We sold 7 St George's Terrace for 16 times what we had paid for it and bought a smaller house in Chiswick. It was in a development on the Thames with a pretty little garden running down to the river and our own landing stage. There was a prolific apple tree on the lawn, a reminder of the days when Chiswick Staithe had been part of the Duke of Devonshire's orchard. Nearly all the rooms, including our bedroom, faced the river. It was a delight to watch not only the Thames flowing up and down but the constant traffic of barges, sailing boats and pleasure steamers.

On holiday in Sardinia where the Aga Khan was beginning to develop the Costa Smeralda, we fell madly in love with the island. Before the holiday was over we had bought a picturesque small house which was being built in the nearby Piccolo Pevero bay. Before the arrival of the Aga Khan the Costa Smeralda was a wild, deserted stretch of coast. In Sardinia the inland mountain slopes were the prime property and were inherited by the sons. The coastline was considered valueless and so was left to the girls. Suddenly there were a host of rich Sardinian girls! Number 3 Piccolo Pevero was one of 12 enchantingly designed little houses cascading down the hillside. Across the undeveloped road it was a few steps onto our own tiny beach, and into the emerald green waters of the Med, where we swam and harvested the mussels off the rocks, to be cooked within a few minutes for lunch and eaten on our patio roof. We bought a power boat and moored it in Piccolo Pevero, and called it *Strauss* because the TV series had paid for it! We bought a Mini and drove it to Sardinia via Genoa, where it was lifted onto the ancient ferry in a precarious net. The Mini was left at the tiny airport in Olbia and there it stayed unmolested for months on end, being picked up only when we or our friends needed it to drive to Piccolo Pevero.

Bill Maynard's star had waned. He was no longer a draw as a stand-up comic. He needed a new career as an actor and joined the Nottingham Rep. Before his career took off again things were not too easy. Bill has never been over-modest in good times or bad. But I warm to him, with his dismissal in injured tones of every objection to his behaviour raised by colleagues, producers and, most of all, writers! During his dog days he was badly in need of a pantomime.

I had just inherited, from a retiring colleague, the representation of Derek Nimmo, who was at that time starring in *Charley Girl* in New Zealand. Derek had been a favourite of the Grades since his early days, when they had employed him as a road manager for visiting American variety stars. Apparently, Lew was so sorry for this undernourished and skinny young employee that he gave him an old overcoat to keep out the worst of the winter weather. Leslie Grade, the youngest and possibly the most dynamic of the three brothers, had suffered a severe stroke, and was now a shadow of his former self. Nonetheless, he was carrying on business and was about to mount *Babes in the Wood*, at the London Palladium. Hearing that Derek Nimmo was now with me, he thought he had a better chance of persuading him to accept a role.

Derek's previous agent, Freddie Joachim, was a legend. He was an accountant by training, and approached show business with slight disdain. He recognised only films and the legitimate theatre as suitable areas in which his clients should work. He dismissed television and possessed neither a radio nor a television set. He had a radio until 1938, when he was so disgusted with Chamberlain's speech after returning from Munich that he threw it out of the window! If he was forced to watch a client on television he asked permission to view the programme at the BBC in Langham Place. His dictum, 'an artiste's greatest asset is his availability', meant that he turned down most work for his clients on the assumption that something better would turn up. No wonder Leslie Grade had difficulty in getting Nimmo to the Palladium. I phoned Derek in Auckland and apprised him of the offer.

'What am I to play'?

'Kind robber.'

He was at the time slightly in awe of his new agent, and accepted my advice, that he would make an excellent 'kind robber'!

'You'll need a bad robber to bully you. Have you anyone in mind you'd like to work with?'

He gave me some names, including most of the distinguished knights of the legitimate theatre, and, not wishing to upset him so early in our association, I promised to check them out and call him back. Bill Maynard seemed a more practical suggestion and he needed the job. He had played the bad robber before, and Leslie Grade liked the idea. I phoned Nimmo again in Auckland, asking him what he thought of the idea of Bill for bad robber. There was a long pause. What I had forgotten was that, in the days when Derek was managing (not as grand a role as the name suggests) a pantomime for the Grades, Bill had been the star and had given Derek a hard time. Derek at the end of the long pause asked me if Bill would be prepared to knuckle down and bully him without stealing his laughs. I should not have reassured him but I did. So Bill was booked to play the bad robber. Bill was summoned to my office before he signed the contract. I made him swear that he would be a good boy and 'feed' Nimmo and that he would treat the role as an acting challenge, and be evil without trying to get laughs.

'Of course, governor, you know me.'

I did and should never have been so naïve.

In December rehearsals started. Derek had pages of material written especially for him. Bill could have told him that it was a waste of time. Kids don't want to listen to people talking – or singing, for that matter. They want the traditional visual gags. Bill dutifully kept his mouth shut. During the dress rehearsal the producer, Bert Knight, rang me at home begged me to come to the Palladium. Unless Derek cut his personal script, the show was going to run over four hours and have very few laughs. Shades of David Jason in Newcastle! Between us we persuaded Derek to cut the dialogue and substitute some business with the bad robber that Bill knew backwards. All was quiet for a few weeks, although Bill's contribution began to become funnier and less evil. There is a traditional scene when the robbers are breaking into the safe. Bill has in his hand a steel wedge and says to Derek, who is wielding a rubber hammer, 'When I nod my head, you hit it.'

Of course the good robber hits not the wedge but the bad robber's head. Apparently, at one performance, Derek reputedly hit Bill so hard and often, not only with the rubber hammer but with the wooden handle, that Bill was knocked out and on recovery jumped into his car and fled to his home in Leicester, claiming concussion! Derek was at first delighted to be rid of him, but, as the days went by, the understudy proved not to have the technique to maintain the success of their double act, and Derek began to pine for his old enemy. Bill was persuaded back ('against doctor's orders, governor') and the battle recommenced.

About a week later two phones rang in the office, Derek on my line, Bill on my assistant's. According to Derek, he had recently acquired a blank cartridge pistol with which he threatened Bill in the duel scene, and then harmlessly fired into the air. Bill had objected, and was refusing to go on for the second house.

According to Bill, however, having already been knocked unconscious by Derek's hammer, he objected to having Derek point his revolver at his nether regions, and was not going to risk having his balls blown off! It was becoming obvious that unless we took immediate action there was unlikely to be an evening performance. I therefore hastened to the theatre. The final scene has a touch of madness. Assembled in a number one dressing room in the world's number one variety theatre were Derek Nimmo, Bill Maynard, Leslie Grade, Bert Knight, the theatre manager, the company manager and myself in serious conference. Having settled, somehow, the matter of the pistol, we returned inevitably to the root of the problem. Whilst Bill was pointing out an apparently invisible, serious, dent in his cranium, Derek was banging me on the head with a rubber hammer as hard as he could, to prove that it would have been impossible to have damaged the unfortunate Maynard! The show went on.

We went into film production in 1973, Ray Cooney, John Chapman, David Croft, Martin Shute and me, Martin being the only one of us with any film production experience. The idea was to make low-budget movies of Ray and John's plays, using the newly developed video camera. We reckoned that with ten days' prior rehearsal under Ray, David could shoot the whole thing in a week! It was a pretty revolutionary idea at the time. We called ourselves Not Now Films as our first film was to be *Not Now Darling*. It was my job to set it up. Tigon films, under a dynamic little producer, Tony Tenser, was at that time churning out low-budget films by the handful. Tony welcomed us with open arms. We were all to work for nothing. Tigon would put up all the money and we were to become partners and receive a lion's share of the profits. Our stars, including Leslie Phillips, Barbara Windsor, Joan Sims and Moira Lister, were offered minute salaries and a share of our profit. It wasn't a bad film at all, in fact it was one of the few Tigon films that worked. When Tigon went broke our immediate thought was that our share of the profit had also gone up in smoke. Happily, however, in drawing up the deal our solicitor had made us partners not of Tigon Films but of Tigon Film Distributors. Film distributors never go broke! We made one more film of an older Ray Cooney farce, *Not Now Comrade*, and Bernie Delfont, now at EMI, backed us, but it was a stinker!

I went to New York again in 1972 and, having just acquired Richard Todd as a client, made a dash worthy of the *Guinness Book of Records*. Richard was appearing in Boston in *The Marquise* with Glynis Johns. I attended a matinee in New York and with the aid of a taxi waiting outside the theatre and the shuttle to Boston from Kennedy Airport, arrived in time for curtain up on *The Marquise*. Richard and I are the same age but he used to receive a telegram each year on his birthday from Ronald Reagan! Reagan and Richard starred together in *The Hasty Heart*, and Richard

113

wrote about their friendship in his autobiography. He sent a copy to Reagan. Disarmingly the President of the United States wrote back saying that he had read the pages about himself, and would read the rest of the book when he was less busy!

My mother died this year. She was over 80. I was never as close to her as I was to my father, but fortunately we had brought her, with her nurse, to stay with us in our new house a few weeks previously and she had so enjoyed looking out of her window at the Thames flowing by, for she was a Londoner.

In the 1970s I was employing mostly men. Now the agency is run entirely by women, who arguably in a small office are better. They are less pompous. When pressed they do their own typing, and always make their own tea. But in those days there was dear old Bill Dickie, the daddy of the office and everyone's father confessor. There was my son Tim, who arrived back from Los Angeles with such long hair it had to be cut off for the more conservative London office. There was Tony Hayes still tapping his way down the corridor. And the not easily forgotten James Kelly — very young, very keen and not yet broken in. He had money of his own and was determined to rid me of mine. Going to see an artiste out of town, I always travelled third-class and walked to the theatre. Not James Kelly. He travelled first-class. When he went to see Peggy Mount in Bath he hired, at my expense, a chauffeur-driven Rolls to meet him at the station to take him all of a quarter of a mile to the theatre. He kept the Rolls and the chauffeur during the play and whilst he took Peggy out to dinner. Then at one o'clock in the morning he rode back in the Rolls to the station, another quarter of a mile! He is broken in now and is a successful executive with another agency.

When Freddie Joachim retired, Derek Nimmo was not our only acquisition. Freddie had apparently asked several casting directors to whom he should 'bequeath' his clients, and I had got the most votes. Freddie only ever represented a maximum of 12 actors, all men. Women, he said, were too difficult to handle. So he wrote to all his 12 men advising them that their careers would be safe in my hands. Warren Mitchell was so incensed at being told where to go, he informed Freddie that although he had already decided to go to Richard Stone, now he was buggered if he would! But Roy Kinnear did come to us. Roy was probably one of the nicest actors that ever breathed, and because of it and of course because of his great talent he never stopped working. Directors loved working with him. Although his comedy television series were consistently mediocre, no one ever blamed Roy. 'Rotten script', 'Bad director', 'Terrible supporting cast', 'Wrong time slot up against *Coronation Street*'. All the excuses that actors make for their failures were made *for* Roy by his employers and they found him another rotten series!

I was golfing on the Isle of Wight, boring my opponent with some of my problems and playing atrociously. Teeing up on the long seventeenth hole I said, 'Now Roy Kinnear, that's something different.' And shot a birdie four! When he so tragically died after falling from a horse whilst filming in Spain, the whole of our profession wept.

We represented Nerys Hughes, one of the Liverbirds. There was no reason why she should escape my 'pantomime net'. She was a name and could earn good money! So Duncan and Paul booked her to play Snow White for two weeks at Torquay. Now Duncan, particularly, was anxious to go upmarket and had just approached Sir John Gielgud to appear for him in a play. He had a lunch appointment with Sir John, and after lunch, brought him back to their newly acquired offices above the Strand Theatre, in what had been Ivor Novello's flat. What Duncan had forgotten was that Paul was interviewing artistes for *Snow White*. Duncan returned with the great Sir John, to find the office afloat with dozens of little men anxious to be amongst the seven dwarfs at Torquay! Sir John did not turn a hair and did the play.

We represented a young actress, Jan Butlin, who sadly died much too young. I worked so hard for her that Peter Saunders spread a rumour that we were having an affair, which we were not! Whilst with me, Jan had a career writing situation comedy, mostly for my clients, and as a director of several West End plays, including two for my shrewd friend Ray Cooney. Barry Took in his book *Star Turns* credits me with being able, if pressed, to sell sand to Saudi Arabia. I am not so sure of this, but I could, if pressed, sell most things within reason to Ray Cooney. But once, overstepping the mark and recommending Jan too strongly when he had already decided to direct a certain play himself, he could take no more and threw the telephone into his swimming pool! One of the plays Jan did direct for Ray was, *There Goes the Bride*, in which Peggy Mount played the grandmother, which turned out to be a fairly thankless part and not nearly so rewarding as that of her husband, played by Geoffrey Sumner. Bill Pertwee, who incidentally was making his first appearance in London as an actor in the same show, claims that Peggy had a 'hate parade' in which Ray Cooney for writing it, Jan Butlin for directing it, Geoffrey Sumner for having a better part and I for getting her the job vied each week for the number one position!

Bill Pertwee tells the tale that, to get him to the audition for *There Goes the Bride*, I went to extraordinary lengths. He was on holiday in Norfolk, playing golf. He maintains that a little man kept popping up from behind the bunkers. Eventually Bill asked him what he wanted. He replied that he had brought an urgent message for Bill to phone his agent!

In the autumn of 1974 a nice thing happened for Sara. Paul Elliot was casting *Cinderella* for Toronto. It was to star Lionel Blair who was also the director. Lionel as a little boy had played Mustardseed in *A Midsummer Night's Dream* when Sara had played Titania to Robert Atkins' Bottom. Some 30 years later Lionel had said to Paul that for the Fairy Godmother he would like a one-time Cinderella like Sara Gregory. Sara had been retired for nearly 20 years and when Lionel rang her, she played hard to get, but couldn't resist Christmas in Toronto with Barry. So off we all went. Sara claims to have set the trend in geriatric Fairy Godmothers, played subsequently by Evelyn Laye, Anna Neagle, Anne Zeigler, Peggy Mount and a new generation headed by Dora Bryan, Gloria Hunniford, Nyree Dawn Porter, Britt Ekland and Wendy Craig.

In 1975 Cameron Mackintosh, then at the outset of his spectacular career, asked me to go and look at a girl in his tour of *Godspell*. The girl was Su Pollard. I was bowled over by her talent and high spirits. One of the first engagements I fixed for her was in a terrible play called *One of the Family*. Peter Rogers, he of the 'Carry On' films had two tame script-writers and they had written a play, and Peter had promised to get it put on. Peter asked me to set it up, and he would back it. Duncan Weldon was still hungry at the time, and welcomed a risk-free venture with open arms. Irene Handl was persuaded to star in the thing, and Su Pollard made her legitimate debut. We opened in Billingham and I well remember tactfully informing Peter that it was customary in theatrical circles for the management to throw a party after the opening night. The information was given to him rather too late and the Billingham Arms could only muster half a dozen chicken sandwiches which had all been eaten before Miss Handl, our star, made her entrance to the party. Su learnt a great deal working with Irene Handl and after *Oh Mr Porter* at the Mermaid and an unsuccessful BBC series, *Two Up Two Down*, I sent her to see Jimmy Perry and David Croft. They gave her what was meant to be a tiny part in the pilot of *Hi-de-Hi!* but it grew. I loved Su Pollard. She was my baby, and I never wavered in my complete faith in her talent.

Sadly, her success gave her illusions of grandeur. I told her she was another Nellie Wallace; she thought she was another Judy Garland. She swore she would never do another pantomime, and she was much too grand to be in another team show for David and Jimmy. She left the office and continued to do David's shows and playing pantomime every year!

Terry Scott had been starring in a very funny farce in London called *The Mating Game*. I had been tempted back into summer season to present Terry in this play after its West End run in Torquay and it had been a sell-out. So muggins here got the bug and agreed to do *Move Over Mrs Markham* the following year. Unfortunately I could not find a good television name to play Mrs Markham. The cast was looking good but with no drawing name. A friend who shall be forgiven told me Tessie O'Shea had expressed a desire on TV to go 'legitimate'. Her agent jumped at the suggestion of her playing the small but telling part of an elderly respectable author of children's books, who becomes unwittingly involved in the sexual peccadilloes of Mrs Markham and friends. The part had been played brilliantly in London by Cicely Courtneidge. For some reason which now escapes me, I discussed the project with Tessie O'Shea on a train to Blackpool. It was a long journey and by the time we got off, Tessie had convinced me that whilst she would love to play the part, her public would be sorely disappointed if she did not sing a song with her ukulele. I needed her name on the posters very badly but there was no way she could sing during the play. So, afraid to lose her, I agreed to have a song written especially for her to sing at the curtain call! Poor Cyril Ornadel obliged once more and we arrived in Torquay armed with a ditty called 'You've Got to Move Over' – not only this but by now Tessie had conceived the idea that whilst she was singing and playing there would be audience participation. The show went well, the audience applauded and prepared to retire to their hotels and boarding houses, or to catch their last buses to outlying districts. But hang on. Whilst the supporting cast stood behind her in mute and acute embarrassment, Tessie produced her ukulele and launched into 'You've Got to Move Over', whilst the fleeing audience were being exhorted to blow up and burst paper bags emblazoned with a picture of 'Two Ton Tessie'. That was my *very* last summer show.

That same year David Croft and Jimmy Perry decided it was time to put *Dad's Army* on the stage. We offered it to Duncan, who was not yet rich enough to present what had emerged as quite a large revue-type musical without some financial help. Fortunately my old friend Bernie Delfont was happy to co-present and put up the money. The show opened in Billingham. It was a good idea to include a chorus and musical items, mainly wartime songs. Ian Lavender was funny singing, 'When Shall I Have a Banana Again?' But the show on tour was a mess. Bernie and I sat at the back of the Shaftesbury Theatre for the first preview in London. It seemed to us that Clive Dunn, bless him, was singing innumerable songs. Bernie was back where he belonged in live theatre, 'sorting it out'. Half Clive's songs were cut, the running order was changed and on the opening night we knew we had a hit. It was in fact one of my happiest nights in the theatre.

The first half finale was 'Home Town', which Flanagan and Allen had sung when they opened the ABC cinema for me in Brussels on the night that city was liberated 30 years before. Arthur Lowe and John le Mesurier sang it now as Flanagan and Allen and the entire company joined them, each carrying a Flanagan and Allen cut-out. Bud Flanagan by now was dead, but Chesney Allen was living in retirement in Sussex. We asked Ches if he would join Arthur Lowe for a surprise entrance on the opening night. He took some persuading and I had to collect him myself from Victoria Station.

117

When he came for rehearsal just before the show, 'Home Town' was not being played in the key that he and Bud had sung it for so many years. There was a quick rewrite in the pit! When Ches strolled on with Arthur Lowe for the encore, the whole audience stood and cheered. It was a great moment. A few years later, Ches came out of retirement and played himself in *Underneath the Arches* at the Prince of Wales.

In the mid-1970s Sara and I took a leisurely trip round the world which included a visit to Sardinia, where I developed a ghastly toothache. An Italian dentist in the local village, on his way out to a game of golf, would only give me painkillers. In Madalena near Porto Cervo there was an American Naval Base. Surely they would have a dentist? I rang them, turned the clock back 30 years and introduced myself as 'Colonel Stone of the British Army.'

'Yes, Colonel, what can we do for you?'

They saw to my tooth, never asked to see any proof of identity and never charged a cent. God bless America!

We stayed in the Oriental Hotel in Bangkok and expected Noël Coward to walk down the elegant curved staircase into the hall. We stayed in the Mandarin at Hong Kong, where Dave Allen was the cabaret. We went to the Melbourne Cup, and met up with both Vic Gordon and Peter Colville, the original comedy act from that first show on Clacton Pier, who had come to Australia in the 1950s and stayed on. After a couple of days relaxing on Moorea in the shadow of 'Bali Hi', we set off for Diana's wedding in Monterey, California. We were apprehensive. Diana had met Rex, a musician, whilst staying with her brother in Toronto, and before settling in California they had spent two years travelling in the Far East. Rex is 6 foot 3 and she carried the pack! They had visited us twice in London and, like many a father before me, I didn't quite agree with my beautiful daughter's choice of a life partner and hoped the whole affair would blow over. But she was in love with him and his music. The wedding in a church in Carmel and the reception up in the mountains were a delight and lulled us into a sense of false security. It took Diana 15 years of marriage and two children to find out that she'd made a bit of a mistake.

Dave Freeman was still in the police force when he started writing bits and pieces for Benny Hill's early television shows at the BBC. He even used to throw off his uniform and work in the sketches with Benny and Pat Hayes. In the intervening years Dave had become one of TV's most successful writers of situation comedy, and had written a great deal for Terry Scott and June Whitfield. Writing weekly television is hard work and Dave is a lazy old thing. He envied the likes of Ray Cooney, who wrote a play every so often, saw it run in London for a year or two, then tour England, South Africa and Australia, each year be mounted in a different seaside resort, and finally be translated and performed in

118

Germany, Holland, France, Italy, Spain, Switzerland and South America. So Dave sat down and wrote a play for Terry and June called *A Bed Full of Foreigners*, and very funny it was too. Terry and June liked it and it opened in, of all unsuitable theatres, the Victoria Palace where it had a good run, transferring later to the Duke of York's. Now Dave Freeman also had a play to tour England, South Africa and Australia, each year be mounted in a different seaside resort, and eventually be translated and performed in Germany, Holland, France, Italy, Spain, Switzerland and South America. So Dave was happy and bought a farm in Kent and didn't need to write for television ever again.

We decided to celebrate Christmas 1976 in Chiswick and invited Tim, his first wife Susan and Susan's parents, Brigadier and Mrs Birbeck, for Christmas Day. Even in the Royal Horse Artillery, Nigel Birbeck was reckoned 'square' so it was with mixed feelings we learnt that Diana and Rex, still letting it all hang out in California, had decided to come over for the holiday. And when Barry, as a surprise, turned up from Toronto on Christmas Eve with one of his more way-out girlfriends complete with a two-year-old baby, indigestion set in long before the Christmas pudding!

It Ain't Arf Ot, Mum, David Croft and Jimmy Perry's next success after *Dad's Army*, had been on the air for a couple of years. It featured an army concert party in Burma, and most of the gang were clients of the office. The most memorable performance was given by Michael Bates as the Char-Wallah. Whereas *Dad's Army* is constantly being repeated, *It Aint Arf Ot, Mum* is on some blacklist for the absurd reason that Michael Bates' loving impersonation of an Indian might give ethnic offence! By the end of the third series Michael was seriously ill with cancer. He could only perform sitting down. For the Christmas season I had gathered together some of my clients from the show and dispatched them to Bradford to perform in *Aladdin* – Michael Bates, Dino Shafeek, Donald Hewlett and Michael Knowles. Donald and Michael, two respected straight actors who played the Colonel and his Adjutant on TV, struggled in Bradford to get laughs as an unlikely pair of English public school Chinese policemen. The experienced Barbara Windsor, playing Aladdin, was not impressed and referred to them as 'those two wankers'.

As the years went by Donald and Michael's act improved, but the name stuck, and around September, managements would enquire if the wankers were free for pantomime! It was during a trip to Bradford that the gang, who all adored Michael, asked if there was anything we could do to give Michael what would probably be his last run in the theatre. Some of them suggested an old Ray Cooney play, *One For The Pot*, in which Michael could play the original Terry Scott part of the old fellow in the wheelchair and Melvyn Hayes could be Brian Rix. So we set it up for a tour and a summer season in Eastbourne. Sadly Michael became too ill to take part, but the tour was already booked. Bill Maynard was free. When I approached him he agreed. 'But I don't want a salary, guvnor. Let me be your partner.'

It was not a wise decision on his part. The play had been a huge success in its day and there had been funny revivals, but ours wasn't one of them. During the interval on the opening night in Worthing the director asked me what we should do. I could only suggest not doing the second half and cancelling the tour – but it was too late.

My managerial forays in the 1970s did not contribute much to the reputation or pocket of my friend Ray. There was *Move Over Mrs Markham* in Torquay, *One For The Pot* on tour, and worse to come. I thought what a splendid idea it would be to turn a Ray Cooney play into a musical – look what had happened to *Pygmalion*. We chose *Not Now Darling* and Cyril Ornadel once again wrote the songs. We decided to try it out a few miles from London – in Johannesburg. Just as well, for every time the cleverly contrived confusion of Ray and John's play was gaining momentum, the actors burst into song and brought the whole thing to a grinding halt. On its return from South Africa we played a couple of weeks in Bromley and Norwich and quietly put it to bed!

Derek Nimmo went into management, presenting dinner theatre mainly in the Middle and Far East. For nearly seven years we helped Derek find the plays, the stars and the supporting casts. They were wonderful tours for the actors, staying in five-star hotels and working maybe only three days a week. In my retirement I sent a memo to Derek:

Richard Stone and Sara Gregory, 'The Colonel and his Lady' surprisingly find themselves vacant following winter in America. No reasonable offer refused. Speak lines. Small parts preferred. Company Management and wardrobe undertaken. Book direct or through any reputable agent.

But we never got an offer. And now, alas, poor Derek is dead following his tragic fall down the stairs in his own house.

I went to Scotland every year at Christmas time for I represented both Rikki Fulton and Jimmy Logan, two of the biggest box office attractions north of the border. Each year Rikki would play pantomime in Edinburgh and Jimmy in Glasgow, and the next year they would change over. They were not always the best of friends and representing them both required the skill of a juggler with a degree in psychiatry! The time spent with each of them must be exactly the same. If I stayed over night with Rikki, then there was no going back to London on the sleeper after seeing Jimmy. I looked forward to their annual appraisal of each other. Rikki is a serious, withdrawn, introverted man, and to him comedy is a precise art, and pantomime should be kept short and neat. He used to ask me each year what I thought of Jimmy's pantomime and then tell me that Jimmy was boring the pants off his audience with a show running for three hours. Jimmy is a typical warm-hearted show business guy and an extrovert. He would ask me what I thought of Rikki's pantomime and again, without waiting for a reply, would tell me that Rikki was not giving them good value as his show only ran for two hours!

Rikki was a splendid actor and had great success with a version of Molière's *School for Wives*, which he called *Let Wives Take Ten*. On the opening night he made a short speech, 'I do not know whether Molière would have approved of what we have done to his play, but I am sure he would have approved of your laughter.'

An elderly woman sitting next to me turned to her friend and asked, in her best Kelvinside accent, 'What's Molly Weir got to do with it?'

Jimmy, on the other hand, spent the summer touring Scotland with his own company in a farce. One year he was presenting Ray's most success-ful play, *Run for your Wife*. I had seen the play dozens of times in England and knew it almost by heart. But so thick were the Scottish accents and so fast did they play it that I could not comprehend one single word!

In 1978 Tim's marriage broke up. On the rebound he told me that he wanted to set up an agency in Los Angeles and would I release him from his partnership agreement with me. Of course I agreed. It was a great blow and I questioned myself for many months as to why it happened. One of the reasons certainly was wanting to be his own man. He had once argued his way in to see the great Lew Grade on some scheme to be greeted with the words, 'Aren't you Dickie Stone's son?'

Tim's version concerns Nimmo again. Tim had already been looking after Derek for me for several years, when they were at a party together. Apparently Derek introduced him to another guest, 'Do you know Tim, my agent's son?'

So, he went with my blessing. It has been a battle for him, but he's still in there fighting.

Victoria Wood joined us in 1978. Vic had been having a rough time. After a regular impromptu song spot on *That's Life* for Esther Rantzen, which had not exactly set the town on fire, she had had a long spell out of work. She was looking for a new agent and sent us some tapes. Lucky us! In my career, spanning by then over 40 years, I had looked after the careers of a lot of artistes. The ultimate staggering success of Victoria Wood was the nicest thing that happened in my final decade as an agent. And Vic herself is one the darlingest people it has been my good fortune to know – and in her case, love. The fact that she not only agreed to write the Foreword to this epic but, despite being in the middle of recording, sent it the next day, perhaps shows that she likes me a little too.

121

There are some golden memories from our first years together, like the script she was pleased to write for Su Pollard who was appearing on Granada's *The Comedians*, and for which Su forgot to pay the agreed fee of £30. And the time I went to see her doing her first one-woman show at the Edinburgh Festival. She was hardly a big deal and so was the last late-night booking in a hall that staged other shows all day. That night she didn't go on until after midnight, and I was due with Jimmy Logan in Glasgow for dinner. She and Geoff insisted on driving me to Glasgow, whereupon a thick fog descended and Geoff walked most of the way leading us with a torch. We arrived chez Logan and, at 4 a.m. though slightly overwhelmed by the baronial atmosphere, they were prevailed upon by Jimmy to share the coq au vin before driving back to Edinburgh at 5 a.m.

It was after her big success with *Talent*, her first play with Julie Walters, that Michael Codron, London's shrewdest impresario, interested himself in Victoria Wood. She was appearing with her husband, 'The Great Soprendo', at the Kings Head, Islington. Geoff, as the Great Soprendo, an immensely funny cod Spanish conjuror, did the first half and Vic the second half. She was so inexperienced then as a stand-up comedienne that I went several times to the show trying to give her confidence enough even to make herself audible. Geoff got the best notices! A few months later, Michael brought *Funny Turns* for a season to the tiny Duchess Theatre, but what with the Falklands war and Vic's then lack of drawing power, the theatre was empty and the season had to be curtailed. Within a very short time Vic became probably the best-loved comedienne in England, a huge star on television and could fill the Albert Hall with her one-woman show.

About now the Americans became interested in Benny Hill. It was necessary to edit his hour shows to 23 minutes for the syndicated market, and to select items from different shows to make up the ideal programmes. Philip Jones and I hit on the idea of engaging John Street, a retired BBC producer, who had worked with Benny in the 1960s to edit, and a great job he made of it. The shows were already being shown before a financial deal had been struck. I was invited to the office of Muir Sutherland, the head of Thames International, at eleven o'clock one morning, and being in Inverness the night before, had to get up incredibly early to catch a minute plane from Inverness to change in Glasgow for the Heathrow shuttle. I was not best pleased when Muir kept me waiting an hour! Had Benny's show been shown unedited there was a clear Equity and Writer's Guild agreement which laid down the rate of payment to him in America, both as a performer and writer, based on his English fee. But there was no rule which governed shows incorporating items from several different pro-grammes. Muir tried, quite rightly, to bluff it out, claiming that each 'composite' programme should be treated as one English show. I had a feeling that even Equity would never agree to that and was sufficiently pissed off

122

Keeping clients at the top of the tree

Every artist will agree that there are agents and agents. RICHARD STONE, whose clients include many of the most distinguished names in entertainment, has been in business for 30 years and, before that, was himself an actor. Here he discusses his philosophy and his approach to his work.

by a Television Today reporter

"IT is fairly easy to answer the telephone and accept engagements for one's biggest clients at the top of the tree," says Richard Stone, probably one of the most influential of London's television agents, summing up the popular idea of the agent's job.

"It is getting them there, keeping them there and helping them to find a new niche when they are slipping a little that requires experience and skill," he adds.

Richard Stone's experience as an agent is spread over 30 years, ever since, after the war and with the rank of lieutenant-colonel, he left the War Office where he had founded the world-wide Combined Services Entertainment (CSE).

His skill owes something to his own personal experience as both actor and variety artist. Leaving RADA in 1939, he worked in repertory, whence he gathered a scrapbook of consistently favourable notices, and in concert party, where he met his wife — the Australian actress and singer Sara Gregory who was with him in the cast of the Little Theatre Cabaret at Saltburn.

Little Theatre Cabaret, for which Richard Stone also wrote the script, was a favourite with pre-war radio audiences in the north; during 1939 it was broadcast three times, under the direction of BBC producer Harry S. Pepper — twice on the north regional wavelength and once from all the regional transmitters.

The beginning

This personal knowledge of the problems of the young performer was put to good use in 1949. Although his career was interrupted by the war, when he fought in the North African and Italian campaigns, gaining an MC on the way, he was still able to put his entertainment experience to good use; and in 1944 he landed on the Normandy beach-heads with six Stars in Battledress companies among whom were Arthur Haynes, Terry Thomas, Wilfred Hyde-White, and Sid Milward and his Nitwits.

He started his agency in 1949, encouraging young comedians by presenting them in summer seasons. Many of those youngsters are now his biggest clients, among them Benny Hill, Dave Allen, Terry Scott, Jon Pertwee and Bill Maynard.

It is the absence of the old type summer show, the seaside concert party, that he blames for the lack of fundamental training and experience for the young variety artists today.

"Harry Secombe, Dave Allen, Max Bygraves and many others all started in these shows. They had no stars, just a talented group of professionals pulling together with nine or so changes of programme in the season.

"The Fol-de-Rols, Gaytime, Twinkle — I booked artists into all of them and they got their training there. They learnt, some of them, to charm the birds out of the trees.

"Today the summer shows are quite different. They feature a known star, supported by others a little less well known and by a few newcomers who keep the ball rolling between the star's appearances. It's not the same thing at all and it's very hard for young artists today to get either the experience or the warmth that these shows generated.

Talent shows

"Some of them go on the talent shows where they are 'discovered' and made into 'stars' long before they are ready for it and it is sad to see them falling by the wayside."

Richard Stone's clients did not fall by the wayside, but as time went on and styles of entertainment changed, most of them no longer wanted to work in the seaside shows. Gradually they moved out of variety into television, legitimate theatre and films.

It became clear that the activities of the agency must change emphasis and Richard Stone concentrated his activities on the form of "packaging" which he now does.

"I feel that, at all levels, my job is now to create packages to the advantage of my artists, writers and directors," he says. "I have a staff of eight superb executives, each specialising in booking artists in different areas of their work."

There are, for example, departments for television drama and for comedy, for television drama and for commercials.

"This," he says, "leaves me free to work at what I regard as creative agency".

He emphasises that his packages are put up solely in the interests of his clients. "I don't get a package fee or anything like that," he says. "I don't often negotiate a complete production. More usually I put together an artist and a writer, or a writer, an artist and a director, and negotiate them together with the idea.

"The rest of the work — casting, design, costumes, music and so forth — becomes the responsibility of the BBC or whichever ITV company has negotiated the package."

Variety artists

For instance, Thames's Whodunnit, created by Jeremy Lloyd and Lance Percival and starring Jon Pertwee, was a package negotiated for three of his clients. Yorkshire's Life Begins at Forty has star, writer and director — Derek Nimmo, Jan Butlin and Graeme Muir — all from the Richard Stone stable.

Although only Jon Pertwee was in fact a client, Richard Stone "sold" the whole idea of Worzel Gummidge to Southern.

He is doubtful whether a new generation of variety artists comparable with those who have for so long held the fort on the television front, is in the offing. He refers back to the difficulty of giving them the background and the experience needed, something that cannot really be obtained by working the clubs.

Only two of his own clients, Benny Hill and Dave Allen, remain in the top flight of variety artists, and he does not envisage them fading out in the foreseeable future.

Situation comedy, he maintains, is a different kettle of fish. It demands the good comedy actor and there is certainly no lack of them, with the resurgence of regional theatre and the work of the Fringe giving the training which a multiplicity of reps large and small used to provide.

New packages

Meanwhile he has at least seven new, major packages in the pipeline including a show with and for Dave Allen.

A new series for Bill Maynard, written by Jan Butlin and to be directed by Graeme Muir is being negotiated. So is a comedy series written by Peter Jones to star Moira Lister and Peter Jones.

"The latter is an example of the way I work what I've called creative agency," he explains. "Moira Lister wanted a comedy series. Peter Jones is a client and was an obvious choice as writer. So I brought the two together and now we have an idea, a writer, the two principal artists and even a title, Mummy and Daddy, that I hope to place as a package."

Peter Jones has also conceived a major historical series which is in process of being sold. A new panel game (all-British for a change) has been devised by Lance Percival and Jack Douglas.

Jack Douglas has another idea, in which he is joined by Tudor Davies, for a musical that could start its life on television. And yet another package being finalised now with ATV is for Jimmy Logan to present his own one-man show as Harry Lauder.

Richard Stone has also represented writers Jimmy Perry, David Croft and Jeremy Lloyd in setting up film or stage versions of three television series — Dad's Army, Are You Being Served? and It Ain't Half Hot Mum.

But the agency goes further afield than London and the regions.

"To make the packaging world-wide," says Richard Stone, "I have opened UK Management in Los Angeles, which is run by my son Tim. With the co-operation of other London agents, he is able to specialise in offering English talent to American television.

Benny Hill

A minor phenomenon in Los Angeles at the moment, says Richard Stone, is the popularity of Benny Hill who has become something of a cult since he was seen every night in last month's Thames Week on the Californian station KHJ-TV.

Benny Hill has steadfastly refused all offers to appear in American television shows. His television appearances remain exclusively on Thames — "and that is entirely due to the treatment he has received over the years from Philip Jones, Thames's controller of light entertainment", Richard Stone says emphatically.

But for the Thames event 35 Benny Hill shows were edited down to five half-hours and these went on in Los Angeles nightly at 11.00pm against CBS news.

"He was an instant success," Richard Stone says. "I think he caught their imagination in just the same way as the English saucy seaside postcard.

"One Los Angeles viewer probably summed up this impression most aptly when she said, at the end of the week, 'Isn't he naughty!'."

©The Stage Newspaper Ltd

to counter bluff. I shut my briefcase and saying, 'Sorry Muir, no deal,' made for the door, knowing full well that we somehow had to strike a deal, since the shows were already transmitting in America. Muir called me back and asked me what I wanted for Benny. My suggestion, off the top of my head, was that we forget all about residuals and split any profit 50 per cent to Thames and 50 per cent to Benny Hill. In fairness, maybe Muir did not quite foresee the bonanza ahead and thought Benny would be on 50 per cent of nothing! In the event, Benny earned as much as £2 million a year, probably ten times what he would have earned under a more conventional agreement. It was certainly my best deal ever.

Our three children seemed now to be settled in the Americas. If we were to spend as much time with them as we wished, our house in Sardinia, much as we loved it, was pulling us in the wrong direction. So we decided to sell. In every sunny haven on earth there is an exile from a colder climate, a mystery man, a Mr Fix-It. George von Lowenstein, to be found in every bar in the Costa Smeralda and at every villa party, was rumoured to be a Polish count with an exciting past. He was tall and good-looking, and bounced around on springy feet. At the faintest whisper of any business deal, George would detach himself from the nearest bar and offer his services to either or both parties. He persuaded us that he would sell our house better than any estate agent and he did!

In October, Sara and I and the banker from Milan who had bought our house came before a notary in Olbia to exchange contracts. It appeared that not only did both parties have to be present, but all the money must be handed over in cash. There was a delay, for our local accountant, one Dr Balata, could not find that any of the houses in Piccolo Pevero had been recorded in the Land Registry. He had sent his secretary to search the files. It was a very hot morning. We all sat in the notary's office waiting for a call. Two hours went by. The notary was visibly wilting, and longing I think for his lunch. For certain in another five minutes he would have allowed the sale without the information about registration. The phone rang for Dr Balata. Had he passed off the call as an invitation to golf or a plea from his mother to visit her in hospital, the sale would have gone ahead by default. But his reaction was one of amazement – 'Impossibile, impossibile' he shouted. It transpired that, due to an oversight, our house did not officially exist! There could be no sale.

We returned to England, and our purchaser to Milan. The cash was returned to the bank. The process of registration was put in hand, and a month later we convened again in front of the same notary, the deal was completed and we left with the cash. When we bought the house we had to buy £2,000 of something called premium dollars for the privilege of taking money out of the country. When we sold, these mysterious premium dollars had risen in value, and a grateful government gave us

124

back £25,000! Within a month Maggie Thatcher came to power and cancelled premium dollars altogether.

Taking things easier we set off on another round the world tour with a business element as the rather feeble excuse. We visited Nimmo in Adelaide, where he was appearing in Ray's *Why Not Stay For Breakfast*. He had a phone-in radio programme and Sara's old friend, Viola Wilson from the Gilbert and Sullivan tour (now Lady Viola Tait), rang in and announced herself to be Lady Longcock — claiming that there were not many Longcocks left in Australia, and other such ruderies. Derek flew Sara and me over Ayers Rock — a hair-raising adventure even though the owner of the plane was by his side! We went on to Perth, where I had arranged a couple of shows for a local impresario, one John Thornton. So impressed was John with the shows that he asked later if he could put my name on his notepaper as his London representative. I never heard from John Thornton ever again!

We came home via India so as to visit the Taj Mahal. There was no moon that night so we settled for sunrise. Before the crowds arrive the Taj Mahal silhouetted against the sky made us two old pros gasp at that incomparable theatrical set. On to Cairo, and tea once again in Groppi's, not changed one iota since 1942, and a taxi to Shepheard's Hotel, which seemed not only different but in the wrong place, until I realised it was a new Shepheard's Hotel!

11

*From producing to packaging, advice from a Hollywood
pro, and celebrating my 50 years in show business*

In my teens I had only one thought – to be an actor and writer. In my
twenties I was firstly involved in fighting a war but later was able to satisfy
my creative urge by organising and producing entertainment for the forces
in Germany and then all over the world. When I decided to become an
agent there had to be something more to life that being a high-class sales-
man. So for 20-odd years my extra energy had been expended on summer
shows. Now that my days as a producer were over, I began to concentrate
on putting together packages. There were the films with David, Ray and
John. There was Worzel Gummidge, first on television and then in the
theatre for a not very grateful Jon Pertwee. If he could possibly avoid paying us his dues, he did!

I packaged tours and summer seasons to unsuspecting impresarios of
plays written by clients and featuring my out-of-work actors. I did the
same thing on TV with the more successful ones. The Head of Comedy at
Yorkshire Television was Duncan Wood, the same guy who, as a fledgling
producer in the 1950s, had given Benny Hill his first radio series on the
West Region only. On the strength of this Duncan and I optimistically set
up a tour of West Country seaside resorts in the depth of winter. We should
have opened on Boxing Day in Weymouth but there was so much snow on
the ground that even the artistes couldn't get to the theatre. Duncan and I
were old mates and now we would have lunch, and I would come up with
my schemes. At one time three out of the four situation comedies produced by Yorkshire emerged from our meetings. And what is more important, they were all hits involving Peggy Mount, Derek Nimmo and Bill
Maynard.

And yet in my dreams I am always still an actor looking for work, or
missing the train call and forgetting my lines on opening night. I once
dreamt that I had two offers. One was to have a vasectomy live on television. I was encouraged to take the job, on being told that there were six

126

episodes with six distinguished people each having a vasectomy, and amongst them Bernard Delfont! I needed the 'exposure' but decided to take the other job as leading man in a provincial rep, thinking that it was more of an investment in my future career. Unfortunately when I arrived at the rep the director apologised that, as I was quite unsuitable for a leading man, the best part he could offer me in his current production was a corpse!

In 1980 Tim was married for the second time. He had done the correct thing and asked Belinda's father, Colonel Alastair Balfour, for his daughter's hand in marriage. Alastair, already in his seventies, appreciated this old-world courtesy, but nevertheless felt the need to make further enquiries. He phoned me from London to the Isle of Wight, introduced himself, and insisted that we must meet. I asked when and he thought later that same day would be suitable. He sounded very impressive and he invited us to have dinner in an Italian restaurant near his London flat. I was putting on my old Carthusian tie when the phone rang again. It was Colonel Balfour suggesting that as this was a serious meeting indeed, it should not after all take place in a restaurant. We were to come to the flat. We crossed the Solent and drove to London. We were as apprehensive as any couple journeying to an important job interview. On our arrival, having lost the proffered Italian dinner, there was no suggestion even of a cup of coffee. It was obvious that Alastair and his wife Elizabeth did not think that a divorced theatrical agent just setting up in Los Angeles was a very good prospect for their only daughter, whom they had hoped would marry Prince Charles!

In April Tim and Belinda were married from the Balfours' beautiful home, Daywick near Peebles. It was a glorious spring day; the grounds were covered in a carpet of daffodils and the trees in Alastair's famed arboretum were at their best. The simple ceremony in Stobs Kirk was very moving. Whatever reservations they may have had, Alastair and Elizabeth gave them a great wedding.

Before the grandchildren began to arrive we had annual family reunions in rented villas in the sunshine. The first was in Puerto Vallarta in Mexico. It was built on the cliffside with nearly 200 steps from the top to the beach. Every 20 steps or so down was a room clinging to the rock face. Sara and I arrived a few days before Christmas in the pouring rain. First impressions were not good. The villa was not looking at its best, and there was no glass in any of the windows! But the sun came out before the family arrived and we realised then that there was no need for glass. Barry as always came with a new girl and got engaged again, but this one lasted an even shorter time than usual. A few weeks later he took her for a holiday to Jamaica. She wanted to lie in the sun, and he wanted action. So he hired a bicycle and cycled round the island. When he got back his girl was married to the hotel manager.

At our Chiswick house we had a real character as a daily help. Cyn was a large, jolly cockney with a loud voice and an equally loud, and almost continuous, raucous laugh. American guests often returned home with a vivider memory of Cyn than of Harrods or the Changing of the Guard. Her husband, Ernie, gave us a bit of help in the garden. We were lucky to have Ernie and Cyn, and Cyn was lucky to have Ernie. She had lived with her first man for over ten years, presenting him with three fine girls. When she found out that his weekends were not, in fact, spent visiting his invalid mother but his legal wife, she threw him out, and advertised in the local paper for a husband. She 'tried out' several applicants, including a major in the army, who was 'much too posh', but Ernie the retired local postman fitted the bill.

Since the fiasco on the *Ed Sullivan Show* Dave Allen had fought shy of America. The rest of the English-speaking world was at his feet. He could be guaranteed to play to capacity audiences with his one-man show in England, Australia, New Zealand and Canada. His television shows, although very badly edited in New York, were having quite a success in the States and were being shown ad infinitum on the Public Broadcasting Service. Encouraged by this, Dave decided to try again. An American millionaire impresario, Jerry Perenchio, agreed at a lunch in Los Angeles with Tim and me to back a New York season. We played it very carefully. Dave did a two-week season in Boston in May to get the feel of an American audience. It went well. Encouraged, he opened in New York in September. The first night audience was ecstatic and we all went in good spirits to Jerry Perenchio's lavish opening night party. But in the early hours, the notices arrived and they were not good. Within minutes the crowded night club was empty and for the second time Dave and I were alone in New York

I had been asked by Derek Nimmo to see if there were any American stars interested in his Middle East tours. With this in mind I contacted an elderly agent, one Ben Pearson. Ben, in his seventies, had his office in Santa Monica manned only by himself and an even more ancient secretary. He made a living booking film stars of the 1940s and 1950s into dinner theatre. In a voice like Schnozzle Durante, he wheeled and dealed like every agent in a backstage Hollywood musical. I sat in his office fascinated whilst he was on the phone to one of his managements.

'Ya can't put Zsa Zsa Gabor into that motel. She'll get raped, and for what you're paying her it ain't worth it.'

Eventually I gained his attention and we were sent to Anaheim to see Cyd Charisse in *Bell, Book and Candle*. Tony Martin, her husband, sat with us through the meal and the performance and hardly stopped reminiscing long enough for me to take in the play. The next morning I phoned Ben and told him that Nimmo would probably like to book Cyd.

128

'Listen, Richard, Cyd Charisse is a rich lady. Nimmo will have to treat her good. Fly her over first-class, put her up at the Savoy Hotel, give her lots of expenses, and it don't matter much what the salary is. But there are others. Take Virginia Mayo, she's a poor widow lady, not so well off. Put all the money on the contract and she'll swim over'.

Bill Dickie had for some time been suffering agony from chronic arthritis in both hips, and had been struggling to the office with a stick. It seems that the strain on his system had been too much and my old friend died.

We thought a celebration in a theatre would have pleased him more than a memorial service. At the Theatre on the Green at Richmond we played Bill's recording of 'Largo il Factotum' from *The Barber of Seville* to a packed house. His brother Murray came from Vienna and sang. Jimmy Logan read Bill's favourite Burns poem, and the audience joined Jimmy as Harry Lauder in 'Keep Right on to the End of the Road'.

My Aunt Dolly, now in her nineties, was living with Catholic nuns in a hospice in Jarnac, where she died. Dolly had told me that she wanted to be cremated and her ashes scattered with my father in the Garden of Remembrance in Cheltenham. The French at this time did not approve of cremation, certainly not in the Charente. The funeral service was still going on when the funeral director knocked on the door of the chapel to ensure that someone was paying his bill before he would remove poor Dolly to Paris, the only city in France where they would undertake a cremation. When her ashes were available they were put on a plane for London, but were treated as freight and Sara spent a day tracking them down at Heathrow. They sat in my study at Chiswick whilst we made arrangements for the scattering. I was telling a young cousin the date of the ceremony on the telephone, when there was a long pause at the other end of the line.

'Have you checked the ashes?'

They didn't, according to Jean, necessarily do a good job in Paris.

'You'd better shake them'.

They did sound a bit solid, so we sent then to Golders Green for further crunching! The final chapter in this black comedy concerned my cousin Adrian, the son of Basil Liddell-Hart and my father's other sister, Jessie, who had died a few years previously. Adrian rang to ask if, as he had still got his mother on the mantelpiece, they could have a joint scattering! Sadly Dolly and Jessie had not been good friends. They had not spoken for 20 years. After carrying out Dolly's last wishes, getting her ashes to England and getting them suitably prepared for Cheltenham, I was not prepared to spoil it all by mingling her with Jessie!

In September 1983 we set off again, for New Zealand, a country I had not seen before, although Sara had played there for six months during the war with the Australian Gilbert and Sullivan Company. We were bound for Invercargill, where Dave Allen was playing the first of three nights. Invercargill is a small, depressing, industrial town on the very bottom of the South Island. The best hotel was in fact a motel on the outskirts of the town, where we joined Dave and the touring manager. It was about five o'clock, pouring with rain, and the streets were deserted. Dave told us it had been difficult to arrange to eat after the show as the only decent restaurant in town normally closed at nine!

In our room was a copy of the local paper, but no advertisement for the show. Later Sara and I took a cab down the main street to a seldom used Theatre Royal. Outside the theatre were posters advertising the visit, in three weeks' time, of the 'Chinese Theatre of Magic'. Not a hint that the curtain was about to rise on Dave Allen. I sought out the theatre manager. Indignantly I asked him why there was no printing, no pictures, not even a mention in the local paper of my client.

'Listen,' he said 'I'm not wasting money like that. We sold out all three performances two months ago when they first heard he was coming.'

We said goodbye to Dave, and drove to Queenstown, where the unpredictable Dave turned up again on his way to some other godforsaken sold-out theatre, and we had dinner. There are very few people in New Zealand and a lot of sheep. If Dave had been a draw with the sheep I reckon he could have stayed at his next one-night stand for a year!

At the Hong Kong Hilton Derek Nimmo was appearing in one of his own shows with Geoffrey Palmer and Barbara Murray. To be entertained by Derek was to enjoy the best of Nimmo. The play was one of Willie Douglas Home's lesser known efforts, *A Friend Indeed*. Whether I was carried away by Derek's hospitality or the convivial reception the play received in the Dinner Theatre, I foolishly, on my return to England, recommended the production to Ray Cooney, whose Theatre of Comedy had recently bought the Shaftesbury Theatre. The theatre was dark awaiting a new production in three months' time so Ray decided to risk a limited season of *A Friend Indeed*. Barbara Murray was not available so Derek asked the Colonel (me) if the Vicomtesse (Moira Lister) could take over. The whole affair was a disaster. Sadly, on this occasion, by recommending it to Ray, I had not proved myself 'a friend indeed'.

Whilst in Hong Kong we made a side trip. In 1983 China was not easy to visit. The Chinese Embassy in London had told Sara that we could not visit in September because China was full! In October there was room, so we went then. We assembled for documentation and briefing with the other 20 or so people who were being allowed in. A volunteer was called for to be our leader. An American hand shot up. In every group there is one person who should not be leader, and in every group he is. I caught the eyes of two charming black ladies, a mother and daughter from

Philadelphia. We giggled and thereafter became close friends. We set off from Kowloon in a hovercraft destined for Canton. It was reassuring to read, on the life jackets and the emergency exits, 'Portsmouth to Ryde Hover Travel'. It was an exciting trip by plane, bus and train. We had no idea where our guide was taking us, or where we would spend each night. We were taken to the circus in Shanghai and courteously offered ice-creams in the interval by our guide. As a setting for the grand finale we were promoted to the bleak Imperial Hotel in the centre of Beijing. Next morning we stood and gazed in Tiananmen Square and wandered through the Forbidden City. I'm glad China wasn't full!

Later that year Sara and I went to St Lucia on our way home to check on a proposed land purchase. The visit confirmed that our lawyer had taken a year's siesta. We stayed the night in the La Toc Hotel, whose beach we had all used the previous year at Christmas. Then having just acquired unman-ageable soft contact lenses in which I was scared to swim, I had lost a lens down a plughole in the hotel changing room. The hotel's West Indian plumber had unscrewed the 'U' bend and rescued it from amongst the slime. I swam again this year and lost the same lens down the same drain. The same amazed plumber enquired if, in my country, this was an annual ceremony!

Late in his career I had acquired as a client Michael Pertwee, Jon's brother, but a much nicer man altogether! Michael was a playwright and had written half a dozen moneymaking farces, most of which had origi-nated with Brian Rix at the Whitehall Theatre. I wish I had represented him in the best years. Now the line of farce he wrote was not so much in fashion. Michael, together with John Chapman, came up with an indiffer-ent piece called, *Look, No Hands*. David Jason, was looking for a West End vehicle and Michael Codron, although having reservations about the play, much wanted to find a vehicle for David. The extraordinary thing was that the funnier David made the play, the more Michael and John were convinced he was ruining their masterpiece!

Anne Knight, who had been running our television department since 1966 and was by far the longest serving member of the staff, died after a long illness in 1984. She was never a very creative agent, and seldom I'm afraid got anyone a job. But she was very good with people. She would talk for hours and hours to anyone with a problem. Bill Maynard, Nicholas Parsons, Pat Coombs each took up two hours of her every working day. She and Bill Dickie died before I formed the partnership. They would have been partners, and both would have liked that so much.

With three diminutive grandchildren, the family Christmas on sunny islands were perforce abandoned. For two years we exchanged our Chiswick home at Christmas for a delightful house in Pebble Beach, near the famous golf courses. It was a short walk to Bird Rock, where hundreds of sea lions sit making a tremendous racket. *'Oink oink'* were the first words our first grandchild Ben uttered. Percy Edwards would have liked such a grandson.

Tim needed a larger house in Los Angeles and moved to Hancock Park, as civilised an area as you can find in Los Angeles, a town with no entity and no soul that I have grown to hate. However, we wanted to see him and his children so the garage at the back of the yard was converted into a one up, one down pad for our visits. Later the same year we bought a house of our own in Pacific Grove 'the last home town in America', a village I have grown to love. The Monterey Peninsula, consisting of Carmel, Pebble Beach, Pacific Grove and Monterey, lets you wake up to 'Another nice day in paradise'! It has beautiful beaches facing north, south, west, and even east, some calm and secluded, and some with great rolling surf. There are magnificent pine forests and our house, built on the side of a hill, looks down across the Pacific. We have a large deck outside the living room built around an old oak tree, and deer wander into our garden and eat our flowers.

With the likelihood of more and more time being spent in America, I had to make a decision about my professional life. The clients and staff had begun to wonder what was happening, and so had I. In May 1986 I formed, with my regiment of women, Meg, Vivienne, Lynda and Irene, the Richard Stone Partnership and agreed to phase myself out over the next five years. In fact we went salmon fishing in Scotland the moment the ink was dry on the partnership agreement!

We had never gone after salmon before, although we had for some years been fishing for trout at Bicton near Fordingbridge, where we had achieved a certain notoriety that very year. Sara had driven our brand-new car and parked it facing a whirlpool in the Avon and didn't apply the handbrake properly. Sitting on the rear bumper to put on her fishing boots, she pushed the car gently into the whirlpool, where it spun happily around. Some lads from the trout farm stripped off and jumped into the water in an attempt to stop it on its way to Southampton. All was going well until one helper shouted to Sara to throw him the keys. He unlocked the door and the car sank! Needless to say, when pulled out by a tractor it was a complete write-off!

Perhaps the most popular of David Croft's shows since *Dad's Army*, *'Allo 'Allo* reached its peak in 1986. We launched the stage show at the Prince of Wales Theatre. It was a huge success and played two further seasons at the Palladium. It was presented by Mark Furness, a young impresario who was perhaps the last of my 'special relationships'. Early in his career he had put on a tour of *Babes in Arms* starring Su Pollard, and I wanted to protect her. Fearing that Mark's tour might be on a shoestring budget, I sent him a cheque for £2,000 to be spent on Su, clothes, microphones, whatever she might ask for and might otherwise not get. The show was a disaster. I had forgotten about the £2,000 and *Babes in Arms* but Mark chose not to forget and gave me, for nothing, a £2,000 investment in *'Allo 'Allo*. It was a nice gesture. I was deeply sorry when a few years later, just as Mark's future seemed assured, he had three major flops in one season and ran into trouble. I was even more sorry when, I think overcome with worry, he died a few years later.

I had become an addict of 'frequent flyer' programmes. Whilst in America I read a Pan-Am advertisement in the *Los Angeles Times*. It appeared that if you flew anywhere on Pan-Am within the next two weeks you could earn triple miles for the rest of the year! We had no plans to go anywhere in the next two weeks but I rang Pan-Am and asked what was their shortest and cheapest flight from LA. It seemed that a day trip to San Diego could cost only 30 dollars and would qualify for the bonanza, so we took our grandchildren to San Diego zoo! We flew so much that year and earned so many triple miles that we travelled free all over the world for the next two years and helped to bankrupt Pan-Am!

Coming back from Scotland in August that year after I'd caught my first salmon, we spent a couple of days in the Lake District at a remote B and B. Victoria Wood and Geoff came over from their home in Grangeover Sands, and Vic and I went walking. We talked not of show business but of family, and what it had meant in my life, and what it might add to hers. Now her two lovely children have done just that.

I accepted an invitation from one of my partners to a drinks party to be held on a boat on the Thames, with but a passing thought that a boat on the Thames was a strange place to have a drinks party, why not in her house? When we arrived and found over 200 of my friends, I discovered that the real reason for the party was to celebrate my 50 years in show business. I was shattered and very happy. My partners had invited dozens of clients, past and present, our two sons from Los Angeles and Toronto, most of the theatrical managers I had dealt with over the years, casting directors and even one of my masters from Charterhouse! It was indeed in November 1938 that I had joined the Croydon Repertory Company as a student ASM. In the 50 years that followed I had been a stand-up comedian, an actor, a soldier, an impresario and an agent, and the company that night had all been with me at different times during that half century of 'frivolity and fun'.

I cannot recall a more momentous year than 1989. We were scarcely back from our winter in America when everything started to go wrong for Benny Hill. For nearly 20 years Benny's relationship with Thames Television had been one of mutual trust. Philip Jones would ask me how many shows Benny wanted to make, and Ben would usually say, 'Tell Philip three, but if I've got enough material we'll try for four.'

With this flimsy information, Philip would fix film and studio dates. The bookers at Thames would then ring me and discuss terms, and the contract often arrived after the filming had already begun. When Philip retired, his job as Head of Light Entertainment was taken by John Howard Davies, who in his first year had rung me to say that Benny's fee was much too low, he was invaluable to the company and must have a large rise! Should I have then viewed this gesture with suspicion? Whilst I was in Scotland in early May, trying unsuccessfully to catch another salmon, I read that John, in Montreux for the Television Festival, had told the press that he intended making sweeping changes in his department and getting rid of most of Philip's long-running comedy successes. Surely this could not include Benny? However, as soon as we returned south, I put in a number of calls to John, whom I had known since he was a boy at Aldro, a little senior to my sons. He never returned one of my calls. I was suspicious but felt partially reassured as the dates for Benny's 1989 shows were already in Thames' schedule, without a contract, in the spirit of the last 20 years.

I was digging potatoes on my allotment when Sara came up to tell me that John had at last returned my calls. I rang him back and he then told me he had bad news. He had apparently just summoned Benny to his office and informed him that Thames were not going to make any further Benny Hill shows. I suspect that John was under orders from his Controller, an intellectual by the name of David Elstein, who considered Benny sexist. It is ironic that Elstein is now the head of Channel 5 and transmitting, presumably in search of ratings, intellectual pornography – a far cry indeed from Benny's innocent bawdy humour. Nevertheless, that John could have sent for his biggest star and dismissed him like a school-boy is unforgivable. Whatever the reason for the decision, John should never have done it this way. He should have taken Ben and me out to lunch and aired his grievances. If the shows were said to be sexist, he could have asked for restraint. If the shows were too expensive, he could have asked for economies. If Benny was suffering from overexposure, there being arguably too many repeats, the solution was in his own hands. If at the end of lunch we had not found a way of continuing, an agreement to part company would have been announced. This would have left me free to explore other avenues, and one of Britain's greatest comedians would not have been sacked by an ungrateful company, which ironically was shortly to lose its licence!

A lot of books were written about Ben when he died. Margaret Forwood, in her book *The Real Benny Hill*, heads Chapter 17 'SACKED', and I quote:

In April 1989 Thames invited Benny to attend the MIP TV Festival, a programme sales market for TV companies from all over the world, held in Cannes. Thames were pushing the boat out at MIP because it was their coming of age. Being paraded in this way was not something he enjoyed, but because he thought it would help Thames, and because it was in the South of France, which he loved, he agreed to go. Thames Television International, the company's sales arm, issued a press release which was positively gushing in its effusiveness: 'Benny Hill, the world's most successful comedian and Thames' longest serving artiste, will be attending the MIP – TV for the first time from Friday 21 April to Monday 24 April as part of Thames Television's twenty-first anniversary,' it began. It went on to describe Benny as a 'world legend in his own lifetime', and 'a genius'. It said that his show had topped TV ratings all over the world and still had audiences 'begging for more'. Only Thames wasn't begging for more, it transpired.

The interview with John Howard Davies had shattered Ben, and he was on the phone to me within the hour. I came to London and we had a sad lunch together in a pub on the river near my Chiswick home. What he could never understand then, or for the rest of his life, was how he could be considered blue with his seaside postcard humour, when some young comics were being obscene on television. He used to count the number of times one comic used the words, 'mother fucker' in one evening.

Something had to be done immediately to restore Ben's confidence and to boost his morale. I turned to the two friends who would not let me down, Philip Jones and Don Taffner, the distributor whose determination had launched Benny in America. Without a moment's hesitation Don committed himself to at least one *Benny Hill Show*, which he would finance personally and hope to sell later. But for two years Thames' action in sacking Benny in this way virtually banished him from British screens. No matter what Philip, Don and I tried to do, we ran our heads against a wall of prejudice, and with no British outlet the show remained a one-off. In that first week the press were bombarding us all. Thames put out a story that Benny was taking a rest. One forceful journalist, being told no-one in my office had any further comment, asked the temporary receptionist her name and began his article, 'Talking to Benny Hill's agent, Sandra...!' Inevitably the truth leaked out and the Sunday papers had a ball. It was some compensation to Ben that in a poll in the *Sunday Mirror* nine out of ten readers wanted him back on their screens.

With only two years before my complete retirement, we felt the urge to put down roots. We sold the house in Chiswick and our holiday flat in the island, and bought Cambisgate in our beloved Seaview. It looks out over our own sea wall with magnificent views across the Solent to the mainland. There is a balcony right along the front with a ship's rail and steps leading down to the garden. With the sea so near, you could well be on board ship. Underneath we converted what had been largely a boathouse, into a self-contained flat, where we installed a charming young couple who hopefully will keep an eye on us in our dotage!

Perhaps this is a good moment for a few Isle of Wight limericks I have concocted.

> There was a young lady from Brading
> who tried to reach Portsmouth by wading.
> When the waves reached her neck
> she said 'Oh by heck
> I think that my chances are fading.'

And a slightly period one:

> There was a young lady from Whippingham
> who like the cold seas with a nip in 'em.
> She covered her tits with two threepenny bits
> and went down to the sea for a dip in 'em.

And my favourite:

> There was an old lady from Binstead
> who I'm sorry to tell you is since dead.
> This is hardly the time
> for a jocular rhyme
> so I'll write an obituary instead.

We now lived on the island and I drove sometimes to London. There were more limericks on the way!

> A stockbroker living in Fleet
> Said what very fine people I meet
> All the nice girls wear jerseys and pearls
> And have sensible brogues on their feet.

> There was a young lady from Hook
> Who could neither embroider or cook
> Nor could she sew
> Or make flowers grow
> But she was a remarkable fook.

It only remained now to have somewhere to stay in London for my rare visits to the office and for Sara to continue her manicures with a Miss

Thomas, which had started in 1942! Rather late in life ex Lieutenant Colonel Stone wished to join 'The Rag' – the Army and Navy Club in Pall Mall. Having been duly proposed, I was vetted by the Secretary. I explained to him that, if elected, we would be staying quite frequently in the club, and I hoped it would be in order for my wife to be visited by her manicurist.

'Oh no, Colonel, I'm afraid we don't allow lady guests in the bed-rooms.'

When I explained that the lady guest was over 80 and had in fact cut Winston Churchill's toenails all through the war, the Secretary decided to make her an exception!

In the throes of our move I had a temporary cash flow problem and was not looking to be 'an angel'. But Paul Elliot and Greg Smith were old friends, so was Laurie Mansfield, a younger agent for whom I have a great respect. Together they were presenting the musical *Buddy*, based on the life of the legendary Buddy Holly. At first I declined to become involved but they kindly claimed that it would not be the same without me, so in went a few thousand pounds. On the opening night of the provincial tour in Plymouth the show was a mess but with great potential. Paul, after giving a few notes, was on his way back to London. I begged him to stay with the show until it was right. It seemed to me to be a celebration of Buddy's songs, and I suggested there was much too much plot, nearly an hour needed cutting from the dialogue. I was not popular with the co-producers or the author, but Paul stayed and cut. The show is still running in London. Maybe it was the last time I was of some slight help to my beloved profession.

My story has been memories of show business. A word to my friends: you may now put this book on the shelf with all your other show business autobiographies and forgive me if you have not been mentioned. The cast list is complete and there remains only a handful of post-production credits.

12

*Gone fishing – sailing round the world, Benny Hill's
death, and life at the Richard Stone Partnership goes on*

All my life I have loved fishing – any kind of fishing. Catching salmon and trout on the fly, deep-sea sport fishing when in the Americas, even out in my old boat in the Solent, spinning for mackerel or drifting with a spoon for flat fish, or, most exciting, trailing a sand eel behind the boat as near as the rocks as we can get and catching bass any where up to 6 lbs. I am perfectly content even to sit on a rock for hours and cast a ragworm into the sea. Now I can do this off my own wall in front of my own house! Two hundred yards across the beach from Cambisgate, so close that it is uncovered on the spring tides, is an outcrop of rocks. It seemed sensible to add a couple more to the lobster pots that were out there each summer. So I bought a little rowing boat that could be winched up and down over the wall onto the beach. I bought two brand-new lobster pots and painted *R.S.* on the buoys. On the day of the launch of the boat and the pots, I was approached on the beach by a teenage youth who offered himself as my mate. We rowed out together and dropped my pots. It was then that he asked if he could pull up some of the other pots. 'That one's mine, that one's my dad's, that one's my granddad's, that one's my uncle's'.

He obviously came from a family of keen fishermen! When we rowed back we were greeted by two ferocious-looking thugs. Richard, the young lad, quickly sloped off down the beach with his purloined catch. The thugs grabbed me by the arm.

'You've been stealing lobsters from our pots. Which would you like? You can give us one of your pots or get a belt round the 'ead you'll never forget.'

I tried to explain that I was an innocent victim, a respectable ratepayer and a senior citizen to boot.

'We don't care if you're in a fucking wheelchair, you're going to get beaten up.'

By now shaking with fear, I finally convinced them that Richard was the culprit and they shot off down the beach in hot pursuit. But someone was after me for the rest of that summer, either the thugs or maybe Richard, for my pots kept disappearing as fast as I replaced them.

After that disastrous year, things got better. Now Sara has replaced young Richard and sits in the bows as ballast whilst I pull in the pots, and Richard and the thugs have gone away. An average of four lobsters a week tends to blur the memory of my rough initiation.

We decided that as long as we kept our health and strength we would travel as much as we could, and we fancied long trips on freighters.

Our first freighter trip was on the *Santa Fe*, a Norwegian ship out of Houston bound for South America. The passengers included an immense American in his seventies who introduced himself with the words, 'I'm Harry Wolf Junior – and I'm a bit of a card.' He certainly was, and a crashing bore. He'd been everywhere, seen everything, known everyone and had the biggest house and the biggest bank balance. He used to fall asleep on his back in the tiny swimming pool, revealing the biggest belly! The other passengers were charming.

In Buenos Aires we took on thirty clapped-out coaches destined for public service in the Dominican Republic. It took a long time to lift them from the dockside and drop them into position in the hold without adding to their already considerable wounds.

We called at Santos on our way back, the port for San Paolo, Brazil's biggest industrial city high in the mountains above. The Brazilians have built two lanes of striking motorway up – but then the money ran out, and the return to Santos was down the precarious mountain road. Our last port of call was Santa Dominico in the Dominican Republic to give them their coaches. To discourage Haitians from the other side of the island hitching a ride to the USA as stowaways an armed guard was posted and a false notice announcing next port of call: Rio.

A great trip – we were hooked.

It was the middle of April 1992 and we were nearing the end of another winter in California when I was told that Benny Hill was dead. My first reaction was to jump on a plane for England. But it was a few days before our Golden Wedding. My brother and his wife were arriving the next day, Barry and Kim (later that year to become his wife) were flying from Toronto, and our house was already bursting at the seams with grandchildren. I felt somehow that I was letting Ben down by not being at his funeral. But, in one lifetime, it would be hard to celebrate 50 years of marriage more than once! I decided that I would make it up by organising Ben's memorial service when we arrived home.

Sara and I reconfirmed our marriage vows at St Marys by the Sea in Pacific Grove. Barry, Tim and Diana stood behind us. I had reserved

139

rooms in our favourite hideaway, the Ventana Inn at Big Sur. High on the hills above the Pacific, it has one of the most idyllic settings of any hotel in the world. Barry and Tim said they had arranged an entertainment for us after dinner and I feared a kissogram! It was in fact a 90-minute video compiled of messages from friends and clients spanning half a century and coming from all over the world. Ian Wallace, my old school friend, raising a glass of whisky in Hampstead. Ian Carmichael, my erstwhile staff captain, raising a glass of champagne in Yorkshire. Anne Ziegler, immaculately coiffured and belying her 80 years, contributing an entire autobiography on tape! Messages from America and Australia and Dave Allen toasting us with a cup of tea from London.

There was a sad contribution from dear Benny in his hospital bed, a few weeks before he died. When he and Sara were very young and met on tour, they had dinner together and Ben asked her back to his digs, but she wouldn't 'come up'. It was a running gag all our lives and now it was on tape.

'Poor Sara, married to him for fifty years. Nice woman but she won't come up'.

It was the last recording Benny ever made.

A Service of Thanksgiving
for the Life and Work of

BENNY HILL

will be held at

St. Martin in the Fields Church

Trafalgar Square, London, WC2N 4JJ.

on Wednesday 23rd September, 1992

at 11 a.m.

For seat reservations, please bring this card with you and register your name with Lynda Ronan
The Richard Stone Partnership, 25 Whitehall, London SW1A 2BS (Tel: 071-839 6421)

We held the Memorial Service for Benny at St Martin-in-the-Fields in late September. Max Bygraves had written, a few years earlier, a song about Benny and he sang it at the service with Benny's backing group, The Ladybirds – it was quite touching that although over the years there had only ever been three Ladybirds at one time, no less than five turned up for the service! I liked Max's gag that, when Frankie Howerd and Benny died, some workmen called out to him, 'Hey, Max, you've let us down, we had you for a treble!'

Patricia Hayes was first on, in second spot and was delightful. Pat must have been in her eighties, and when we rang her a few days before to remind her she had said, 'Oh, the Benny Hill Memorial. Haven't I done that yet?'

I read out some messages we had received. Perhaps the best was from Jack Lemmon;

> From the age of seven or eight I fell in love with the great masters of comedy, such as Chaplin, Keaton, Laurel & Hardy, W. C. Fields and a handful of others. As I grew older a few others gained my great admiration, but in recent years my favourite above all was Benny Hill. He was a master in his field ... he could be broad without going 'over the top', willing to take chances and most of the time being successful at it, and where most comics and comedians might deliver a barrage of powder puffs, Benny could give you a cannon shot. I miss him.

And finally, Anthony Burgess paid tribute to Benny's talent and I shall always remember one phrase, 'I speak primarily as a common man who, like other common men and women, recognised a richness of talent that was invisible only to the mirthless, the prejudiced, and the stupid.'

It was in 1995 that we took our second freighter trip on a British ship, *The Forthbank*, sailing round the world. We only joined for the middle segment from Papeete to Singapore, scheduled to call at ports in the Pacific Islands like Samoa, Fiji, Noumea, The Solomon Islands, New Guinea, Australia and The Philippines. It was scheduled for seven weeks, but in the event lasted eleven. One of the main reasons for the delay was caused by the pilot coming out of Honiara in the Solomon Isles. He managed to hit the jetty with the propeller! We limped into Oro Bay in New Guinea – the back of beyond with a jetty for only one ship. Engineers flew in from London and New Zealand and the cargo was moved to the front of the ship to raise the stern and the offending bits were cut off the four blades of the propeller.

On Sunday, we walked in a temperature well over 90 degrees a couple of miles to the nearest native village, a collection of huts on stilts by the sea. They were holding their church service on the beach. Prayer books, hymn books, seats and a mat were brought for Sara and me. After the service we were thanked for coming and the whole village lined up and filed past us to shake hands! We felt like Royalty.

From Darwin to the Philippines we passed through the China Straits and a warning notice was circulated:

141

PIRATES

For some time now, Merchant Vessels trading in the South China Sea, Singapore Straits, Malacca Straits and Indonesian waters have been subjected to attacks by Pirates. Theses usually operate from small fast boats not readily detected by Radar. They often approach from astern and nearly always target the Master's accommodation area, where they expect to find money or valuables in the safe. There have however, been instances where other crew on board have also been robbed of money and valuables. In addition, apart from the usual knives etc, they may also be armed with guns. It is the policy of the British Government and Andrew Weir Shipping Ltd. that in the event of the vessel being boarded, a non-violent response is taken.

The majority of pirates and armed robbers are opportunists seeking an easy target and time may not be on their side, particularly if the crew are aware they are on board and are raising the alarm with the Authorities.

For these reasons, security will be strictly observed at night in these waters as per the attached arrangements.

Please be assured that we all take this risk seriously, your co-operation will be appreciated.

Yours faithfully

P.G.H Stapleton
Master

I wrote a couple of limericks on this trip!

> There was a young man from Noumea
> Who was a remarkable pee-er.
> At his very best
> With the wind in the west
> He could drown a whole town in Korea.

And my favourite!

> There was a young man from Raboul
> Who had a remarkable tool.
> No, it wasn't that kind
> You've an 'orrible mind
> What on earth did they teach you at school?

142

There have so far been two more freighter trips. The first round New Zealand and up to Korea and Japan. The second from New Orleans through the Panama Canal to the West Coast of South America, visiting Colombia and Equador. By now, dear reader, you will, if you have survived, have learnt enough about freighters! Just a brief note or two then and all down for the finale!

On both trips we encountered huge storms. A typhoon on the way to Korea was carefully bypassed by our old captain – a younger captain in charge of the sister ship lost all his cargo overboard. On the South America trip coming home during El Nino we met the worst storm I have ever known. For a time we dared not leave the cabin as everything hurtled from side to side. Every time the ship hit a wave, even when the speed had been reduced to 4 knots, the ship banged and shook as if we had hit a rock!

Two things made the Korea–Japanese trip memorable. We arrived in Busan (the only two passengers by the way!) on a Saturday afternoon, unable to speak a word of the language or to read any signs. I got in conversation, however, with the radio operator of a Russian ferry, which unbelievably brings Russians from Vladivostock for a weekend shopping in South Korea! So important and economical is this that one street has been renamed Russia Street. This nice fellow escorted us for two hours in Busan, through the crowds of shoppers, mostly in a subway at least a mile long, and Sara got her hair done in an upstairs room in a store with at least 30 women all being seen to at once by 15 or so girls – while I sat patiently in the midst of it all playing with a Korean child. By now we knew which way we were facing and how many underground stops it was to get back to the ship.

One of our goals in Japan was to find a golf club in Kobe where Sara's father had captained the team in 1912.

We started from Osaka. A monorail and two trains later we reached Kobe. In the square we quizzed some Japanese businessmen. The oldest golf course was apparently on the top of Mount Rokkosan. So back one train, one bus, one cable car, and we are at least up the mountain. But the golf course is another 2 miles up! No transport until a kind man in a Mercedes gives us a lift. The course is closed for the winter, the chairs in the club house are all piled up but on the wall is a picture dated 1912 of the competing teams Kobe and Yokohama and there is Sara's father! Mission accomplished.

Sadly that's the end of our freighter trips as with no doctor on board they won't take passengers over 80, which we both are! But in 1999 with another couple of old friends we rented a boat on the Burgundy canals. So here are, I promise, the last two limericks:

143

A pretty young harlot from Beaune
Booked all her clients by phone.
But her favourite cat
Pulled the phone out and that
Left her several evenings alone.

There was a young girl from Auxerre
Who had a remarkable pair.
She took up the slack,
Tied them both at the back
And strangled herself on the chair.

Maybe I should have written a book of rude limericks and forgotten about the autobiography.

But we are still enjoying life flying between our homes in California and Seaview. We can still go fly-fishing and rowing out to the lobster pots, still work in our allotment and I can still play a round of bad golf!

I'm quite proud that, eleven years after my retirement, the Richard Stone Partnership is flourishing. Vivienne Clore, arguably the best and most influential agent in the field of light entertainment, manages amongst others Johnny Vaughan, Rory Bremner, John Fortune, Jo Brand, Mark Thomas and Richard Whiteley. For my old clients David Croft and Jimmy Perry she arranges fabulous repeat fees for all their hits including *Dad's Army* (none of their shows are still available free to the BBC!)

Meg Poole on the drama side has an enormous stable of actors including Simon Russell Beale and Roger Allam, both acknowledged to be two of the best actors, if not the best, of their generation. David Jason has stayed happily with Meg, as has Bill Maynard. Lynda Ronan, amongst other things, copes with the estate of Benny Hill, whose shows are still showing all over the world (except England – 'a prophet is without honour in his own country'). They bring in a lucrative income which then has to be divided amongst the six beneficiaries under his will, the children of his late brother and sister, three in Australia, three in England. And they all have to be consulted before any new deal is struck!

I think we've lived in the best century so far. Early on life was much simpler, when you picked the listening part of your telephone off its hook, the local operator came on the line. When you asked to be put through to Uplands 448, she'd say 'They're not at home, dear. They've gone to Cornwall for their summer holiday.' Today you press a lot of buttons and a recorded voice gives you ten options, none of which you want, so you stay on the line for a customer service representative, who are all dealing with other customers. After half an hour of commercials, music and information of all the things they can do for you, a human being actually speaks to you. But you should not have rung this number in the first place — your query is dealt with in their Aberdeen office. So you start all over again!

Mechanically I have just moved into the twentieth century (not the twenty-first yet) by installing an answerphone in England and a fax in America. Two of each would be going too far! I also have, in a box in England, a mobile phone — one day soon I'll get it out and see how it works. Computers are definitely not on.

Showbusiness must still be fun, but I think I'd miss the old camaraderie, the weekly rep and booking all those comics on variety bills.

Well, that's about it. It's been a great life so far. I thank God every day for my good health, my good fortune, my children, my grandchildren and above all for Sara. We've been allowed to be together for more than 60 years so far and hopefully our names will not be drawn out of the hat for a little longer.

INDEX

147

151